All About Roses

Written and edited by
James K. McNair

Designed by
Craig Bergquist

Photography by
William Aplin
Martha Baker
Clyde Childress

Illustrations by
Ron Hildebrand

Contents

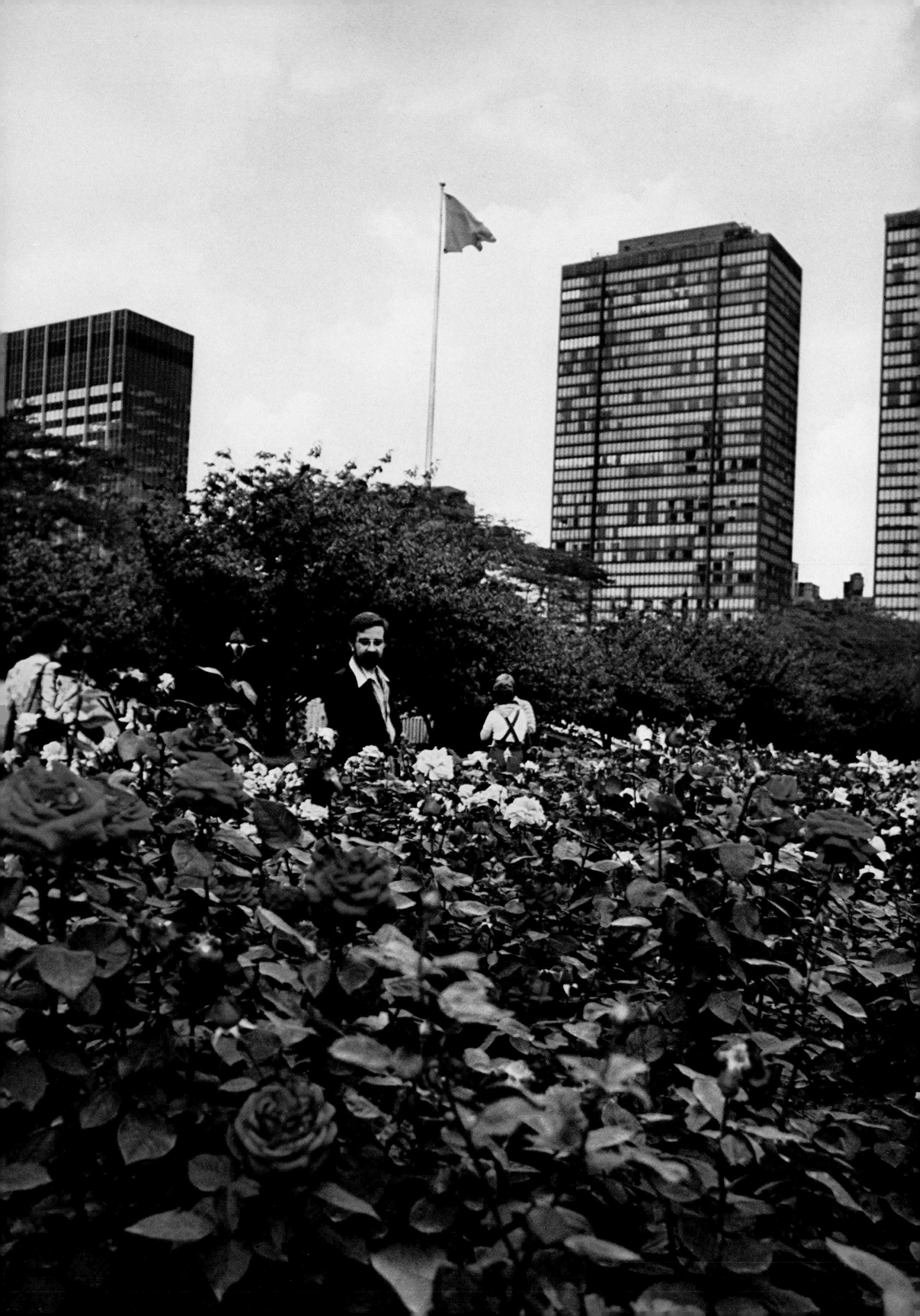

Landscaping with roses

Incorporate varied forms of roses into your landscape design, and you'll be rewarded with long seasons of blooms for years to come.

of the known roses of her day. The fame of Josephine's beautiful formal landscapes spread throughout Europe, and soon everyone wanted roses for his own garden.

Today the rose is certainly our most popular flower. Over 50 million American families have at least one rose bush under cultivation. In the majority of gardens, the roses are not a part of the total landscape design, but are grown primarily for their flowers.

It seems unfortunate that more attention isn't given to the use of roses in the art of landscaping, for no other plant produces so many flowers over as long a period of time. And the variety of plant-growth habits and flower form is mind-boggling.

Roses range from tiny miniatures to towering climbers, with all sizes and shapes in between. They can be formed into trees, trained into pillars, grown into huge shrubs, massed together as ground covers, or planted alone as colorful accents. The flowers offer a rainbow of color and an endless variety of sizes and fragrances.

You don't have to wait years for results to show, because most roses bloom the first year they're planted. And no other plant family grows under so many different climatic and soil conditions. Best of all, they are easy to grow and their care requires only a little amount of time in comparison to the many rewards they return.

Designing with roses

Whether you serve as your own landscape architect, or use the services of a professional, consider some of the ways roses can fit into your landscape.

✓Foundation plantings in various heights around the house make the structure look like it belongs on the site.

✓Massed floribundas and miniatures in beds create a lush spot of color against a green lawn. (The plants will be easier to care for if you raise the beds.)

✓Borders of low-growing roses around flower beds, vegetable gardens, or in front of shrub groupings give long seasons of bloom, and

Roses have always been a part of nature's landscape design. Fossil evidence shows that roses have been around for at least 30 million years. Some type of rose has been discovered growing wild in almost every habitable place in the northern hemisphere of our planet.

Man has cultivated roses since antiquity. Babylon's hanging gardens included roses in the design. The "queen of flowers" came to Western Civilization from Persia. The Greeks cultivated rose gardens, and the Romans spread plantings throughout the reaches of their empire.

When the Dark Ages came, the Church frowned upon roses as a pagan emblem, but ironically the flowers were kept alive in monastery gardens. The Crusaders brought more roses back to Europe. Like other things of beauty, the rose was once again looked upon with favor during the Renaissance.

But it was not until the time of the Empress Josephine, wife of Napoleon, that the rose was restored to its rightful place of honor among flowers. The Empress established extensive gardens at Malmaison with plantings of over 250 varieties, including most

◁

Our cameras visited rose gardens of varied sizes and designs from coast-to-coast. Here the camera explores the United Nations Rose Garden in New York City.

A mass of low-growing floribundas adds a band of color to divide the green lawn from the cement parking area.

save a lot of replanting of bulbs or annuals.

✔Small rose bushes are good rock garden accents.

✔Mobile containers of roses are ideal for patios and terrace gardens, or even to bring indoors when they're in bloom.

✔The placement of roses can create illusions that carry the eye to another point, add extra height, or change the depth of the lawn.

✔Formal or casual moods can be created through plant selection and a planting plan.

✔A grouping of roses or just one large specimen can be used to mark an entry way.

✔Rose-covered screens give privacy combined with beauty.

✔Roses can form a living fence, hedge, or barrier to block a view, give privacy, or redirect traffic.

✔Foreground or background plantings of roses emphasize other shrubs and flower companions.

✔A walkway or path lined with roses invites exploration.

✔Roses can camouflage fences, unattractive structures, refuse areas, sharp angles, or poorly designed architectural features, and they won't inflict structural damage like ivy often does.

✔Well-designed lawns become interesting when edged with roses.

✔Colorful blooms can fill in a corner to give the lawn a completed look.

✔Proper placement of roses can define a specific area of the landscape and focus attention there.

✔Plantings that frame a large window at the bottom and sides can visually bring the rose garden indoors.

✔Raised or recessed beds built into the patio or terrace bring the roses right into the entertainment area.

✔Specimen plants of any form of rose, thoughtfully placed, will accent any spot in the garden.

✔Terraced plantings on a steep slope create a wall or bank of flowers.

If you choose to group roses together in a ''rose garden'' you have a choice of formal or casual styles. Either way can be large or small. It's all in the design and plant selection.

Formal gardens are generally symmetrical, often with geometrical planting patterns. The plants usually follow straight lines. Carefully blended colors are characteristic of formal rose gardens. And often there's some tall feature in the center of the

Prize roses in a cutting garden share space with usual backyard clutter. Owners Tom and Louise Coleman, both American Rose Society Consulting Rosarians, recently won King of the Show at an ARS national show.

planting—a statue, pergola, fountain, or a tree rose—surrounded by roses in descending heights.

An informal garden is achieved by irregular spacing of the plants and flowing lines, providing a natural effect. There may be more colors and varieties combined, and roses are often planted with many other flowers. Roses blend beautifully with any flower you can name.

Consider planting a separate cutting garden, which can serve two functions: it's easier to provide the extra care necessary to grow specimen blooms; and it allows you to leave flowers on the landscape bushes until they fade. Cutting gardens are usually placed out of sight of the public view.

Good designing with any plant material requires an understanding of the particular plant's needs and potentials. Study the characteristics of any given rose bush and how you can expect it to perform in determining where to place it in your landscape design. Consider its height, growth habits (bushy, spreading, upright), and foliage type and color. Rely on pruning to help control how the plant fits into the design. And remember to choose varieties with long-lasting flowers.

If you plan to do your own landscape, make your plans on paper first. By taking this preliminary step you will anticipate and avoid many problems which would otherwise be costly and time consuming, not to mention unnecessary hard work.

There are many good books devoted to the art of landscaping, or you may write your State Cooperative Extension Service (see page 25) for material they have available on home landscaping. The principles of good design are the same for roses as for any other flowering shrub.

Let's consider color

Most people feel that all roses blend together; but some prefer a more carefully worked-out plan to eliminate color clashes and create harmony. Roses will give you a long seasonal parade of color, so plan a look you can live with. Let your imagination decide what colors will fill your garden. It's a matter of personal preference and taste.

You may choose to create a monochromatic scheme by planting roses of a single color, or several shades of one color. If so, choose a hue that blends well with the materials or color of the house, such as all shades of pink with a pink-toned brick house, or an all-white rose garden with a white frame house.

Carefully worked-out blends of two or three colors are preferred by some people with such shades as yellows and oranges planted together, or pinks and reds. You may choose to grow two contrasting colors, such as lavender and orange, or yellow and red.

If you have enough space, use bold splashes of color in every hue. You'll have a riot of color—perhaps more than you want—so temper it with a white rose for a quiet accent.

Mixed colors lose their effectiveness in small areas, so it's usually best to plant three bushes of the same variety.

Bright, warm colors planted at the rear of the garden make the space appear smaller; cool colors make the garden seem longer, or deeper.

Most blooms show best against a background of dark greenery or a dark painted fence or wall. Some deep rose tones, however, need a light-colored backdrop if you're going to enjoy their rich colors.

Whatever color scheme you work out, plant to have color at different levels. Use tall-growing grandifloras or climbers for height, with lower growing floribundas and miniatures to achieve blooms on several levels. Plant height varies within each group of roses; there are short, medium, and tall varieties of hybrid teas, for example.

A few words of caution

Choose your planting sites carefully. Sunshine and good drainage are critical factors in rose growing. Give the bushes and roots plenty of room to develop (see pages 43-46).

Buy quality plants, and keep the quantity to a number that you can cope with, according to the amount of time and energy at your disposal. Be sure you are willing to provide the care that roses require all year long in order to produce a season of blooms. They are easy plants to grow, but will require at least an hour or so of your time each week.

Remember that roses are deciduous, and for the winter months will be only naked silhouettes in most landscapes, or mounds of winter coverings in cold areas.

Don't overplant. The purpose of good landscaping is to enhance the view, not overwhelm it. And don't forget the view from inside the house looking out.

Many colors of hybrid teas are planted together in a large rose bed.

A blend of pink and red roses grows informally with rose-colored phlox in a monochromatic scheme accented with white alyssum.

White House head gardener Irv Williams, right, guided our editor through the traditional rose garden adjacent to the President's Oval Office.

Seaside cottages completely entwined with climbing roses have become a tradition on Nantucket Island, Massachusetts.

Climbing polyantha, Mme. Cécile Brunner, frames this old-fashioned picture postcard entrance gate.

In Berkeley, California, we found a house almost covered with climbing roses and surrounded with an informal rose garden.

Consider planting tradition

Traditional uses of roses in the landscape may mean something different to each of you. Perhaps your first image is of the formal garden style, typical of European estates since the days of the Empress Josephine.

Or maybe you hold a romantic vision of the proverbial rose-covered cottage, a favorite red climber spreading over a whitewashed picket fence, or even trim rows of rose bushes standing at attention in an isolated rose bed.

When you plan your landscape design, think about including some of the best elements from our rose-garden heritage that fit into your own contemporary surroundings and life style.

A formal pergola is adorned with the "thousand beauties rose," Tausendschön, 1906.

All photos on this page show the Huntington Botanical rose gardens, beautiful landscape design that blends formal tradition with informal English country gardens with both old roses and new.

The Shakespeare Garden features the roses and other flowers of Elizabethan time, and those that were mentioned in the writings of the dramatist. Above, Shailer's Provence, right, Petite de Hollande; both are Centifolia roses.

Roses stand out beautifully against a cornfield and form the background for a bed of petunias.

Climbing roses can be trained into pillars with a strong support, judicious pruning, and tying.

This Northern California tree rose has been pruned only slightly in the past 20 years.

A circular bed of roses provides a splash of color in the middle of the paved parking area.

The form of the rose is repeated by the poppy companions alongside a weathered fence.

Try something different

Don't restrict your roses to the rose garden. Give these handsome, hardy plants a chance to perform varied landscape duties. They are far more versatile than they're often credited with being. Place them in the foreground or background, to perform as a colorful star or to blend subtly alongside annuals, bulbs, other shrubs, even vegetables.

The great rosarian is not afraid to experiment—whether it's with new varieties, new methods of culture, or new landscape possibilities. Our travels turned up quite a few good ideas and successful garden designs, as evidenced here and throughout this book.

Pink miniatures and floribunda are planted as companions to provide repeated bloom on several levels.

This weeping Margo Koster tree rose is formed with the aid of a wire frame.

A wise rosarian allowed this hardy white shrub rose to cover two dead trees, forming a canopy for outdoor entertaining. The roses are never pruned.

A rose-lined pathway welcomes you to the Marshall's home.

Mary Marshall stops to admire the little rose named in her honor.

Climbing Peace is a showy background for the cutting garden area.

Climbing Shot Silk covers an extension to the rear of the house.

Small landscape gem

Don and Mary Marshall are both Consulting Rosarians for the American Rose Society and are active rose show judges. When you approach their home, it's obvious that the owners love roses. Our camera captured a part of their garden which is one of the best examples of landscaping with roses that we have seen.

The Marshalls have been growing prize-winning roses at their San Mateo, California home for about 30 years. The relatively small yard contains over 350 rose plants, but is organized with a sense of design. Since both work daily, the garden chores are restricted to early mornings and weekends.

In 1970 Ralph Moore named one of his best miniature varieties for Mary Marshall.

The lawn becomes a bouquet of blooms on all levels.

Miniature rose Sunny Day grows successfully as a hanging basket plant.

The mobile rose garden

When you grow roses in containers you have total freedom to change the design of your landscape for special occasions, according to changes in the weather, or just on a whim.

Miniatures are obvious container-garden candidates, but full-sized roses, even climbers and trees, can be successfully grown and moved in large pots or tubs. (See pages 46-47).

Container gardening is the answer for people with limited space, balconies, decks, or terraces who still want to grow roses.

Container-grown roses can be grouped together to provide colorful gardens wherever they are desired.

An imaginative gardener used a hollowed-out weathered log as a container for miniatures.

An urban high-rise garden

A rose garden in the sky is not some romantic daydream, but a fact of life for Linda Yang. Her very real garden is nestled on two terraces of a modern highrise apartment building.

Ms. Yang long admired roses, but assumed that they could only be grown in country gardens. In spite of discouragement from nurserymen, she has discovered by trial and error that it is possible to add the queen of flowers to her garden.

Her secret is to start with plants already growing in cardboard containers. She avoids buying bareroot roses; transplanting causes too much shock for rooftop growing. She makes her selections at local nurseries and transplants them into her large containers in midspring.

A feeling of slight formality is created on one terrace. A long planter and screen of dark green *treillage* forms the background for climbing roses. The screen also provides privacy from adjoining highrises and protection from cold winds, but does not block the great view of the park. Ivy is a natural choice for ground cover in such a setting. Tree roses are planted in boxes near the apartment windows for an eye-level splash of summer color.

The garden design of the other terrace is quite informal. Climbing roses are trained on a wire fence to frame the cityscape and soften the harshness of adjacent buildings. Floribundas are planted at the bases of the climbers to give rose blooms on all levels.

Hybrid teas and more climbers are grown in large tubs as accent plants. They apparently do not object to sharing the tubs with small but compatible woody shrubs, such as cotoneaster and pyracantha, with an everchanging display of annuals—alyssum, marigolds, and zinnias.

The skyline rose garden is enjoyed by family and friends as a retreat from noisy city streets as well as for outdoor dining. Outdoor lighting creates a pleasant, dramatic effect at night when the terrace is viewed from inside the apartment; quite an unexpected treat for guests in the midst of a great city.

Linda Yang is author of *The Terrace Gardener's Handbook* (Doubleday).

◁

Climbing roses on the 19th floor frame the cityscape and soften the harsh white brick high-rise.

Above: Climbing Don Juan and floribunda Gene Boerner team up for a refreshing contrast to the concrete city below.

Right: The birds are invited to stop and dine among the terrace roses.

Below: A screen provides intimacy as well as protection from harsh city winds and noises.

When the accent is on roses

Sometimes the key word in landscaping is *restraint*. A single strategically placed rosebush can be a bold accent in the garden design. It can serve as a focal point or dominant element; call attention to a particular area; or add interest to a lawn, flower bed, or grouping of shrubs.

When a rose stands alone it needs to be special, with qualities that make it a perfect example of the type of plant it represents. Whether it's a large shrub species, a tree or standard, a spectacular climber, or a hybrid tea of an unusual color, it should be planted so it can be viewed as an individual rosebush or where it will stand out among the other plants in the area it is used. Naturally, a plant given such prominence, must always be healthy and well groomed.

Right: The focal point in the corner of this lawn is a brilliantly hued climber entwined around the gaslight.

A specimen tree rose stands sentinel near an entrance and offers a splash of color to enrich the plain brick wall.

Such a mammoth shrub rose would dominate any landscape. Here, it is wisely used at the driveway entrance.

Roses used in the landscape don't have to be numerous or massive in size to command attention. This single well-groomed species combines colorfully with iris at left. Note the contrast of the giant pink blossoms against the expanse of green lawn.

Visit a public rose garden

You can learn a great deal from visits to public rose gardens. There, you'll discover landscape-design ideas, see new introductions and tests, preview future All-America Rose Selections, smell and touch unusual or hard-to-find varieties, and study old-fashioned species. All show off their best qualities in response to the particular climate of the garden.

Look for roses you like. Observe their growing habits to see how the plants can fit your own landscape needs. Let specimen blooms guide you in selecting the color, fragrance, and size you want for your own cutting garden. Jot down the names so later you can order or find the species or variety that does just what you want. A resident horticulturist is usually happy to answer any serious questions.

We've included a sampling of some of the 250 North American public rose gardens. A complete list with addresses is available from All-America Rose Selections, P.O. Box 218, Shenandoah, Iowa 51610.

In addition, many commercial rose growers have display gardens at their home offices. Check the list on page 26 and call ahead to be sure they have areas open to the public.

United States

CALIFORNIA
Arcadia, County Park Rose Garden
Berkeley, Municipal Rose Garden
Fresno, Municipal Rose Garden
La Canada, Descanso Gardens
Los Angeles, Exposition Park Rose Garden
Oakland, Morcum Amphitheater of Roses
Riverside, Fairmont Park Rose Garden
Sacramento, Capitol Park Rose Garden
San Diego, Balboa Park
San Jose, Municipal Rose Garden
San Marino, Huntington Botanical Gardens
Santa Barbara, City Rose Garden and Armory Gardens
Visalia, Tulare County Courthouse
Westminster, Civic Center Rose Garden
Whittier, Rose Hills Memorial Park

COLORADO
Denver, Denver Botanic Gardens
Longmont, Memorial Rose Garden

CONNECTICUT
Norwich, Memorial Rose Garden
Waterbury, Hamilton Park Rose Garden
West Hartford, Elizabeth Park Rose Garden

DISTRICT OF COLUMBIA
Washington, Shoreham Hotel Rose Garden

FLORIDA
Cypress Gardens, Cypress Gardens

GEORGIA
Atlanta, Greater Atlanta Rose Garden, Piedmont Park

HAWAII
Kula, University of Hawaii, College of Tropical Agriculture

IDAHO
Boise, Julia Davis Park
Lewiston, Memorial Bridge Rose Garden

ILLINOIS
Chicago, Grant Park Rose Garden and Marquette Park Rose Garden
Highland Park, Gardener's Memorial Garden
Libertyville, Cook Memorial Rose Garden
Peoria, Park District Rose Garden, Glen Oak Park Conservatory
Wheaton, Robert R. McCormick Memorial Gardens

INDIANA
Fort Wayne, Lakeside Park Rose Garden
Richmond, E. G. Hill Memorial Rose Garden, Glen Miller Park

IOWA
Ames, Iowa State University Rose Garden
Bettendorf, Community Center Rose Garden
Cedar Rapids, Huston Park Rose Garden
Davenport, Van der Veer Park Municipal Rose Garden
Muscatine, Weed Park Memorial Rose Garden
Shenandoah, Mount Arbor Demonstration Garden
Waterloo, Byrnes Park Memorial Rose Garden

KANSAS
Manhattan, Kansas State University Rose Garden
Topeka, E.F.A. Reinisch Rose and Test Garden, Gage Park

KENTUCKY
Louisville, Kentucky Memorial Rose Garden

LOUISIANA
Baton Rouge, L.S.U. Rose Test Garden
Many, Hodges Gardens
New Orleans, Pauline Worthington Memorial Rose Garden, City Park
Shreveport, American Rose Center

MASSACHUSETTS
Westfield, The Stanley Park

MICHIGAN
East Lansing, Michigan State University Horticulture Gardens
Lansing, Francis Park Memorial Rose Garden

MINNESOTA
Duluth, Duluth Rose Garden
Minneapolis, Municipal Rose Garden

MISSOURI
Cape Girardeau, Rose Display Garden, Capaha Park
Kansas City, Blue Ridge Mall Rose Garden and Laura Conyers Smith Memorial Rose Garden
St. Louis, Missouri Botanical Rose Garden

MONTANA
Missoula, Memorial Rose Garden, Sunset Park

NEBRASKA
Lincoln, Municipal Rose Garden
Omaha, Memorial Park Rose Garden

NEVADA
Reno, Municipal Rose Garden, Idlewild Park

NEW JERSEY
Bloomfield, Brookdale Park Rose Garden
East Millstone, Colonial Park Rose Garden

NEW MEXICO
Albuquerque, Prospect Park Rose Garden
Hobbs, Community Rose Garden, Lea General Hospital

NEW YORK
Brooklyn, Cranford Memorial Rose Garden, Brooklyn Botanic Garden
Buffalo, Niagara Frontier Trial Rose Garden, Humboldt Park
Flushing, Queens Botanical Garden
Ithaca, Cornell University Rose Garden
Newark, The National Rose Garden
New York, United Nations Rose Garden
Rochester, Maplewood Rose Garden
Schenectady, Central Park Rose Garden

NORTH CAROLINA
Raleigh, Municipal Rose Garden

OHIO
Columbus, Park of Roses and Ohio State University Rose Garden
Mansfield, Kingwood Center
Wooster, Ohio Agricultural Research Center

Rose Hills Memorial Park, Whittier, CA.

OKLAHOMA
Muskogee, J. E. Conard Municipal
  Rose Garden, Honor Heights Park
Oklahoma City, Municipal Rose Garden,
  Will Rogers Park
Tulsa, Municipal Rose Garden,
  Woodard Park

OREGON
Corvallis, Municipal Rose Garden,
  Avery Park
Eugene, George E. Owen Municipal
  Rose Garden
Portland, International Rose Test Garden

PENNSYLVANIA
Allentown, Malcolm W. Gross Memorial
  Rose Garden
Hershey, Rose Gardens and Arboretum
Kennett Square, Longwood Gardens
McKeesport, Renziehausen Park
  Arboretum
Pittsburgh, Mellon Park Rose Gardens
Reading, Municipal Rose Garden
University Park, Penn State University
  Rose Garden

SOUTH CAROLINA
Orangeburg, Edisto Rose Garden

TENNESSEE
Chattanooga, Municipal Rose Garden,
  Warner Park
Memphis, Municipal Rose Garden,
  Audubon Park

TEXAS
Corpus Christi, Rose Society Display
  Garden
Dallas, Samuell-Grand Municipal
  Rose Garden
El Paso, Municipal Rose Garden
Fort Worth, Botanic Garden
Houston, Municipal Rose Garden
San Angelo, Municipal Rose Garden,
  Civic League Park
Tyler, Rose Garden Park

UTAH
Fillmore, Territorial Statehouse Rose
  Garden, Old Capitol State Park
Nephi, Municipal Memorial Rose Garden
Salt Lake City, Municipal Rose Garden

VIRGINIA
Arlington, Memorial Rose Garden
Roanoke, Mountain View Garden

WASHINGTON
Bellingham, Fairhaven Park Rose Garden
Chehalis, Municipal Rose Garden
Seattle, Woodland Park Rose Garden
Spokane, Rose Hill, Manito Park
Tacoma, Point Defiance Park Rose Garden

WEST VIRGINIA
Huntington, Ritter Park Rose Garden

WISCONSIN
Hales Corners, Boerner Botanical Garden,
  Whitnall Park
Madison, Olbrich Park

Canada

BRITISH COLUMBIA
Victoria, The Butchart Gardens

ONTARIO
Niagara Falls, Royal Horticultural Gardens
Windsor, Jackson Park Rose Garden

QUEBEC
Montreal, Connaught Park Rose Garden
  and Memorial Park Rose Garden

Brooklyn Botanic Garden, Brooklyn, NY

Municipal Rose Garden, Berkeley, CA,
Below: International Rose Test Garden, Portland, OR

A guide to genus *Rosa*

Roses from ancient species to modern hybrids, including descriptions and sources of many that you should consider growing.

The rose has long enjoyed universal appeal, unequaled by any other plant form. The plants have been prized as ornamental shrubbery for centuries. And the flowers, bathed in the romantic language of love, are present on many important occasions of our lives.

Roses have been immortalized in every form of the arts. They are favorite subjects of painters, poets, playwrights, musical composers, sculptors, craftsmen, and designers. Shakespeare probably spoke for most of the artistic community when he penned, ''Of all the flowers, methinks a rose is best.''

Roses have played important roles in history since ancient civilizations. Probably the most famous role was in the English Wars of the Roses, when the House of York adopted a white rose as its emblem, opposed by the red rose symbol of the House of Lancaster. When the two families merged their differences, a new Tudor rose that blended red and white became the national emblem of England. Roses have appeared on the emblems, awards, currency, and postage stamps of many nations.

Botanically speaking, all roses belong to the genus *Rosa,* a member of the family *Rosaceae.* Relatives include almonds, apples, peaches, raspberries, and strawberries. The genus *Rosa* contains about 200 species, with countless crosses that have produced thousands of cultivars, hybrids, or varieties.

◊

There's something for everyone in the world of roses. Perhaps no other group of plants offers such a vast array of form, size, color and fragrance.

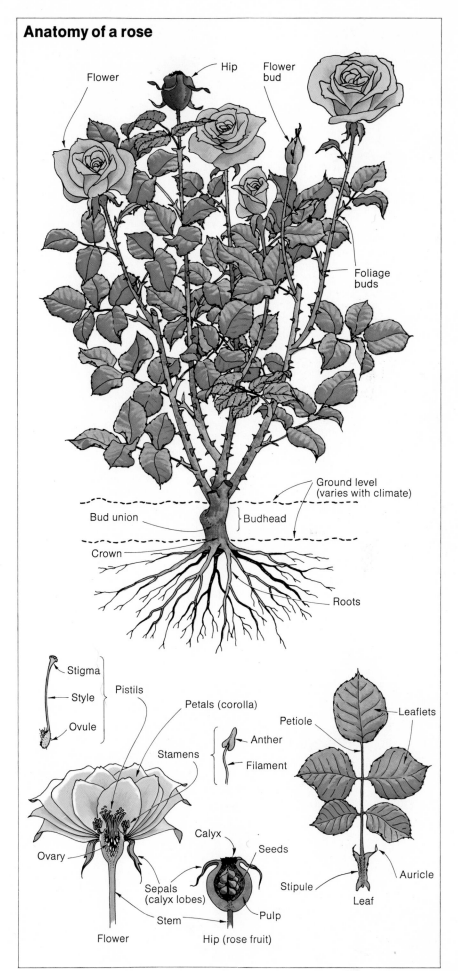

Anatomy of a rose

Flower · Hip · Flower bud · Foliage buds · Ground level (varies with climate) · Bud union · Budhead · Crown · Roots

Stigma · Style · Ovule · Pistils · Petals (corolla) · Stamens · Anther · Filament · Petiole · Leaflets · Ovary · Calyx · Seeds · Sepals (calyx lobes) · Stipule · Auricle · Stem · Pulp · Leaf · Flower · Hip (rose fruit)

Roses from B.C. to the future

At the Huntington Botanical Gardens in San Marino, California, horticulturist John MacGregor has established a very fine collection of roses representative of the genus from ancient times to the present. We invite you to join us on a walking tour through the history of the rose.

GALLICA. We begin at a planting of the oldest cultivated European roses, the Gallica, or French roses. *Rosa gallica officinalis,* often called "the apothecary's rose," predates Christ. It was used in making medicines and fragrances in France. The plants are hardy and bloom once each year in the spring or early summer. Flowers may be single, semidouble, or double in form, with 5 to 100 petals each, according to variety. They are in shades of deep red through purple, to pink and are sometimes marbled or striped with white. Most have a strong, long-lasting fragrance.

DAMASK roses are ancient Mediterranean plants recorded in Egyptian history, cultivated in Greece and the Roman Empire. Summer Damask, *R. damascena* and other varieties are once-blooming; the Autumn Damask, *Rosa x bifera (R. damascena semperflorens)* frequently makes a repeat blooming in the fall. Medium-sized double or semidouble flowers grow in large clusters in various shades of pink to white. All are very fragrant; *R. d. trigintipetala* has been grown for centuries to make attar of roses, the purest distillation of rose oils. Plants are hardy and disease-resistant, with tall, thorny, arching, rather weak canes.

Rosa x bifera, *B.C.*

R. centifolia, *before 1500 A.D.*

ALBA roses are descendants of *Rosa gallica,* crossed with forms of the Dog Rose, *R. canina. R. alba* was known before 100 A.D., and later became very popular during the Renaissance, often seen in Italian paintings of the period. The plant is hardy and both pest and disease-resistant. Flowers are medium-sized, delicate, and fragrant, in shades of pink and white. They bloom once annually in late spring.

CENTIFOLIA. Those huge, very fragrant flowers belong to Centifolia roses, probably a cross of Alba and Damask, produced by Dutch hybridizers before 1500. *R. centifolia* is the "cabbage rose." Centifolias come in every size, from tiny miniatures to 5-inch globes, usually pink with deep centers. Blooms once a year in late spring or early summer.

MOSS. About 1696, sports of the Centifolias, known as the Moss roses, appeared. They resemble their parents except for a soft, mossy growth covering the calyx and stem. If you touch it, you get a sticky, fragrant resin on your fingers. The plants are quite hardy. Some of the Hybrid Mosses were bred from the Common Moss and repeat-blooming Damask and China roses.

CHINA AND TEA. A big boost to European rose development arrived from China in the late 1700's and early 1800's. Forms of *Rosa chinensis,* known as China roses made their debut, followed closely by the first tea rose, *R. odorata.* Chinas have small semidouble blooms in red or pink, with an occasional white streak, and a peppery fragrance. Tea roses smell much like freshly crushed tea leaves, and are medium-sized to large, in pink, cream, and pale yellow. Both are everblooming, somewhat tender plants.

The addition of these repeat-blooming roses created a lot of excitement among the breeders. Advancement was slowed because of the difficulty in crossing the genetic differences in the European and China roses. However, within a few years, many new forms of roses were developed. First to appear were the PORTLAND roses, derived from the Autumn Damasks and Chinas around 1800.

Rosa gallica officinalis, *B.C.*

R. alba, *before 100 A.D.*

Common Moss, about 1696.

R. chinensis mutabilis, *before 1914.*

Jaune Desprez, Noisette, 1830.

R. chinensis viridiflora, *1855.*

Variegata di Bologna, Bourbon, 1909.

Francis E. Lester, H. Musk, 1946.

BOURBON. But it was the Bourbon roses that became the most popular new European rose class. They resulted from a cross of Autumn Damask and Pink China. The repeat bloomers have medium, double flowers in shades of pink to red. The plants are compact and vigorous. Hybrid Bourbons are similar, but bloom only once annually.

HYBRID PERPETUAL. The parentage of Hybrid Perpetual roses is complex, involving repeated intercrossing, among the Portlands, Bourbons, Teas, and Chinas. Hybrid Perpetuals became the rage of the mid-1800's, when at least 4,000 varieties were introduced. Many are still available and worth growing because they are strong, hardy, vigorous plants, blooming profusely in the spring; repeating modestly through the summer, producing large flowers in varied forms in shades of crimson, pink, purple, and white.

NOISETTE. The first hybrid rose to originate in the United States was the Noisette of the early 1800's. It is a repeat-blooming, rather tender climber descended from the Musk rose, *R. moschata,* crossed with China

and Tea roses. It blooms in large clusters of soft pastels.

HYBRID MUSKS. In the 1920's the Hybrid Musks were introduced. These sprawling shrubs or moderate climbers are later repeat-blooming versions of Noisettes crossed with *Rosa multiflora* ramblers. They are very disease-resistant and fragrant and will take more cold than the Noisettes.

HYBRID TEA. In 1867, J. B. Guillot of France bred La France, considered at first to be a more compact-growing Hybrid Perpetual. Similar roses, however, appeared more and more frequently from breeding Hybrid Perpetuals and Tea roses. Soon they were classified as Hybrid Tea roses.

In 1900, Joseph Pernet-Ducher added the yellow strain of *R. foetida*

Two Hybrid Perpetuals: Reine des Violettes, 1860, and a white Mabel Morrison, 1878.

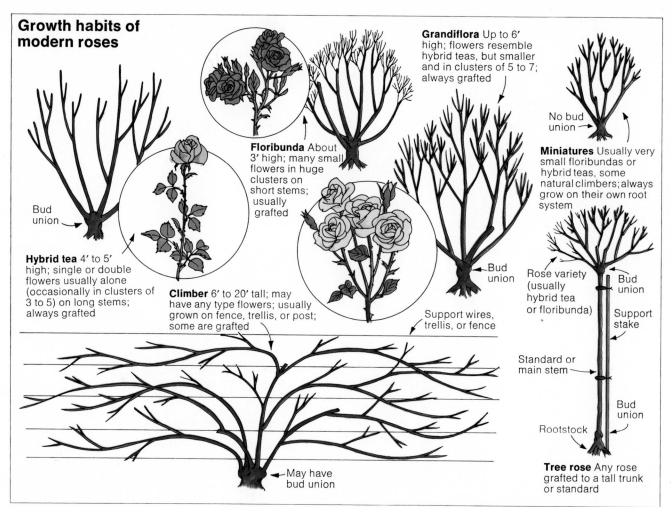

Growth habits of modern roses

Bud union

Hybrid tea 4' to 5' high; single or double flowers usually alone (occasionally in clusters of 3 to 5) on long stems; always grafted

Floribunda About 3' high; many small flowers in huge clusters on short stems; usually grafted

Climber 6' to 20' tall; may have any type flowers; usually grown on fence, trellis, or post; some are grafted

Grandiflora Up to 6' high; flowers resemble hybrid teas, but smaller and in clusters of 5 to 7; always grafted

No bud union

Miniatures Usually very small floribundas or hybrid teas, some natural climbers; always grow on their own root system

Bud union

Support wires, trellis, or fence

Rose variety (usually hybrid tea or floribunda)

Bud union

Support stake

Standard or main stem

Bud union

Rootstock

Tree rose Any rose grafted to a tall trunk or standard

May have bud union

---

to the Hybrid Teas with his Soleil d'Or, opening many new possibilities for hybridizers. For a number of years his brightly colored roses were known as Pernetianas, but were absorbed into the Hybrid Tea class by the 1930's.

Hybrid Teas have undergone constant improvements, until they have become *the* rose of the mid-20th century. Flowers are borne singly on long stems or in small clusters. Colors range from whites through lavenders, pinks, yellows, oranges, and reds, with mixtures and blends all in between. Most are fragrant. Plants are grafted onto vigorous shrub root-

Soleil d'Or, 1900, founded the Pernetiana class and brought bright yellow to Hybrid Teas.

stock to produce salable plants faster in large quantities. They grow from 2 to 6 feet in height and are continuous blooming.

POLYANTHAS arrived on the French scene about the same time as the Hybrid Teas, derived mainly from *Rosa multiflora* and crossed with Tea and China roses. The low-growing, continuous-blooming plants produce large clusters of small flowers in all rose colors.

FLORIBUNDAS, sometimes called Hybrid Polyanthas, resulted from an early twentieth-century cross of the Polyanthas and Hybrid Teas. As the name implies, they produce "flowers in abundance." Blooms resemble Hybrid Teas in form and color range, and are borne in clusters. Most plants are disease-resistant, hardy, and low-growing.

GRANDIFLORA roses came into being about 25 years ago as an American classification to designate roses that are intermediate in habit between Hybrid Teas and Floribundas. The flowers resemble Hybrid Teas, but are borne in clusters like Floribundas. Growth habit resembles Floribundas, but the plants are generally taller than Hybrid Teas.

MINIATURE roses came to Europe about 1815, with *R. chinensis minima* (*R. roulettii*). They were a rage in France, but fashion changed, and they quickly faded from sight. It wasn't until the late 1920's that the miniature was rediscovered growing in a window in Switzerland. In recent years the small plants with tiny flowers have become increasingly popular. Most bloom continuously and varieties appear in all the colors and forms of hybrid teas, with 5 to 70 petals. They have little or no fragrance.

CLIMBING roses and ramblers are botanically tall-growing (6 to 20 feet) plants of any one of the other types of roses. They are not true climbers, since they have no tendrils with which to attach themselves, but must be tied to a support. In the wild, thorns act as tendrils. They may be everblooming or once-blooming each year, and come in a wide range of flower color, size, and form.

SPECIES AND SHRUB. Throughout our historical walk we note interspersed species or shrub roses which played a part in the development of modern roses. Many are native species that grow wild in all parts of the northern hemisphere. Others have been carefully bred and improved through

R. chinensis minima,
Miniature, 1815.

Fru Dagmar Hastrup (Frau Dagmar Hartopp), Rugosa, 1914.

Austrian Copper, R. foetida
bicolor, *before 1590.*

the years. Most are hardy, often resistant to pests and diseases, and are valuable additions to any landscape. Note some of the most beautiful and important ones that follow.

SWEETBRIERS, *R. rubiginosa (R. eglanteria)* and its hybrids, have scented foliage reminiscent of ripe apples. The vigorous plants produce 8- to 12-foot arched branches that are quite prickly. Pink, red, or yellow blooms appear once each year in late spring or summer, followed by an abundant crop of colorful hips.

RUGOSAS are all derived from *R. rugosa,* and produce large hips, valuable for their vitamin C. The foliage is rough and ribbed. Plants are very hardy with fragrant flowers.

NEVADA is a modern shrub with big, nearly single blooms in flesh to pure white, sometimes splashed with red.

CHESTNUT rose, *R. roxburghii,* comes from China. Its buds resemble chestnut burrs.

AUSTRIAN COPPER, *R. foetida bicolor,* is a colorful wild shrub brought to Europe from Persia by the Moors in the 13th century.

FATHER HUGO ROSE, *R. hugonis,* is a beautiful shrub with pale yellow single blossoms, discovered in 1899 by Father Hugh Scallon in China.

KORDESII. William Kordes developed an important collection of modern shrubs and semiclimbers in Germany, from the Sweetbriers and Rugosas. The plants are extremely hardy with a variety of flower forms and colors.

A look toward the future

As we've seen from the development of the genus, roses are not static. There has always been change. Who knows what innovations await discovery, ready once again to change our way of thinking? Perhaps a new type of rose that would overshadow or improve our present popular classes. Such roses are already under development. And there's even talk of a change in the method of classification of the existing roses. But "a rose by any other name would smell as sweet."

R. hugonis, *Father Hugo Rose, 1899.*

Whatever the future brings, we can look forward to more progress in the development of roses—but we must not forget the great roses of yesterday that have inspired artists, lovers, priests, and scientists.

R. rubiginosa (R. eglanteria), *the Sweetbrier rose, prior to 1551. Left, closeup of fragrance glands on petiole and leaf margins. Right, hips in snow.*

Plant a new old rose

If you've ever been intoxicated by the heady aroma of an old rose, then you'll want at least one heritage plant in your garden. Space does not permit listing all old roses, species, and newer shrubs that are available today.

But we asked John MacGregor of the Huntington Botanical Gardens of San Marino, CA, to prepare a list of some of the best cultivars from each of the major categories of old roses that are suitable for a beginner's collection. He advises to start with the first one or two from each group in the accompanying list, if you wish to establish a broadly representative old rose collection. Planting all the listed selections from any one group will give you a good representation of the range of variation within that group.

Ipsilanté, Gallica, 1821.

Frühlingsmorgen, H. Spinosissima, 1942.

Henri Martin, Old Red Moss, 1863.

Locating old roses

All of the roses in our list are available from commercial sources. The following nurseries offer from one or two to many old roses. The availability varies from year to year. There's some disagreement as to correct names, so it may be necessary to try several sources for the plant you want. Write for a current listing; see page 26 for names and addresses. Sources: 9, 10, 12, 18, 26, 59, 62, 63, 64, 65, 66, 67, 69, 71, 77, 82, 83, 84, 87, 89, 90, 91, and 92. European nurseries are excellent sources if you're willing to keep the plants under a two-year quarantine as required by law.

Most old roses are easily propagated from cuttings (see pages 64-65) of plants growing wild, or planted in old gardens and cemeteries. For additional sources, contact botanical gardens that have an old rose collection.

Heritage Roses is a new group for those who grow roses of yesterday. A $2 annual membership entitles you to four newsletters, plus help in searching for ''lost'' or hard-to-find roses or books. Write to one of the individuals listed below for further details.

Edith Schurr, 1315 Ninth Avenue North, Edmunds, WA 98020.

Miriam Wilkins, 925 Galvin Drive, El Cerrito, CA 94530.

Carl Cato, Heritage Roses, 5916 Hines Circle, Lynchburg, VA 24502.

Lily Shohan, Heritage Roses, R.D. 1, Clinton Corners, NY 12514.

A collection for beginners

Gallica
Rosa Mundi *(R. gallica versicolor)**
Tuscany Superb*
Belle de Crécy*
Charles de Mills*
Ipsilanté*

Damask
Rosa x bifera *(R. damascena semperflorens,* Rose of Castile, Autumn Damask)* (R)
Mme. Hardy*
Celsiana
Leda (Painted Damask)
Marie Louise

Alba
Maiden's Blush
Königin von Dänemark*
Félicité Parmentier*
Mme. Plantier*
Celestial

Centifolia
R. centifolia bullata
Petite de Hollande*
Rose de Meaux*
R. centifolia cristata (Crested Moss)*
Tour de Malakoff

Moss Rose
Communis (Common Moss)
Deuil de Paul Fontaine* (R)
Salet (R)
Henri Martin (Old Red Moss)
Gloire des Mousseux

Portland
Rose du Roi* (R)
Comte de Chambord (Madam Böll)* (R)
Jacques Cartier (Marquis de Bocella)* (R)

Bourbon
La Reine Victoria (R)
Souvenir de la Malmaison* (R)
Mme. Ernst Calvat (R)
Louise Odier (R)
Honorine de Brabant (R)

China
Old Blush* (R)
R. chinensis mutabilis (R)
Archduke Charles* (R)
Hermosa* (R)
Louis Philippe D'Angers* (R)

Hybrid Perpetual
Baronne Prévost (R)
Ferdinand Pichard* (R)
Paul Neyron* (R)
Frau Karl Druschki (R)
Heinrich Münch (R)
Henry Nevard (R)
Baroness Rothschild (R)
Reine des Violettes (R)
Georg Arends* (R)
Ulrich Brunner Fils (R)

Tea
Monsieur Tillier* (R)
Catherine Mermet* (R)
Maman Cochet* (R)
Duchesse de Brabant* (R)
Climbing Sombreuil (R)

Noisette
Maréchal Niel (R)
Aimée Vibert (R)

Hybrid Musk
Buff Beauty (R)
Kathleen (R)
Prosperity (R)
Cornelia (R)
Lavender Lassie (R)

Rugosa
Fru Dagmar Hastrupp (Frau Dagmar Hartopp)* (R)
Hansa* (R)
Sarah Van Fleet* (R)
Schneezwerg* (R)
Delicata* (R)

Species
Rosa rubiginosa (Eglantine)
R. foetida bicolor (Austrian Copper)
R. moyesii
R. hugonis (Father Hugo Rose, Golden Rose of China)
R. glauca (*R. rubrifolia*)

Shrubs (Species Crosses)
Harison's Yellow
Golden Wings* (R)
Nevada (R)
Frühlingsmorgen
Stanwell Perpetual* (R)

*Moderate growers which may be easily maintained to a size no larger than the average hybrid tea, suitable to small gardens.

(R) *Reliable repeat bloom.*

Select roses that are best for you

Learn to make competent decisions on rose varieties you want to grow. Consider the type of blooms wanted and your landscape requirements. Check gardens in the neighborhood and observe which roses perform best. Contact local garden clubs and rose societies for suggestions about varieties suitable to the area. Visit public rose gardens where a wide range of roses are displayed. Spend a few winter hours poring over rose descriptions in mail-order catalogs. (See list on page 26.)

Consult our charts on pages 28-41 for descriptions of readily available commercial roses. Call your County Agent or write the State Cooperative Extension Service for published lists of variety recommendations that grow well in your state.

AL　Coop. Ext. Service
Auburn University
Auburn, AL 38630

AK　Coop. Extension Service
University of Alaska
Fairbanks, AK 99701

AZ　Coop. Ext. Service
Univ. of Arizona
Tucson, AZ 85721

AR　Coop. Ext. Service
Univ. of Arkansas
Box 391
Little Rock, AR 72203

CA　Public Service
University Hall
Univ. of California
Berkeley, CA 94720

CO　Bulletin Room
Colorado State University
Fort Collins, CO 80521

CT　Agricultural Publications
University of Connecticut
Storrs, CT 06268

DE　Mailing Room
Agricultural Hall
University of Delaware
Newark, DE 19711

FL　Bulletin Room, Bldg. 440
Univ. of Florida
Gainesville, FL 32601

GA　Coop. Ext. Service
Univ. of Georgia
Athens, GA 30601

HI　Publications Distribution Office
Krass Hall
Univ. of Hawaii
2500 Dole Street
Honolulu, HI 96822

ID　Mailing Room
Agricultural Science Bldg.
University of Idaho
Moscow, ID 83843

IL　Agricultural Publications Office
123 Mumford Hall
University of Illinois
Urbana, IL 61801

IN　Mailing Room
Agricultural Admin. Bldg.
Purdue University
West Lafayette, IN 47907

IA　Publications Distribution Center
Printing and Publications Bldg.
Iowa State University
Ames, IA 50010

KS　Distribution Center
Umberger Hall
Kansas State University
Manhattan, KS 66502

KY　Bulletin Room
Experiment Station Bldg.
University of Kentucky
Lexington, KY 40506

LA　Publications Librarian
Room 192, Knapp Hall
Louisiana State University
Baton Rouge, LA 70803

ME　Dept. of Public Information
PICS Bldg.
University of Maine
Orono, ME 04473

MD　Agricultural Duplicating Services
Univ. of Maryland
College Park, MD 20742

MA　Coop. Extension Service
Stockbridge Hall
University of Massachusetts
Amherst, MA 01002

MI　MSU Bulletin Office
Box 231
Michigan State University
East Lansing, MI 48823

MN　Bulletin Room
Coffey Hall
University of Minnesota
St. Paul, MN 55101

MS　Coop. Ext. Service
Mississippi State University
State College, MS 39762

MO　Publications
B-9 Whitten Hall
University of Missouri
Columbia, MO 95201

MT　Extension Mailing Room
Montana State University
Bozeman, MT 59715

NE　Department of Information
College of Agriculture
University of Nebraska
Lincoln, NE 68503

NV　Agricultural Communications
University of Nevada
Reno, NV 89507

NH　Mail Service, Hewitt Hall
University of New Hampshire
Durham, NH 03824

NJ　Bulletin Clerk
College of Agriculture
Rutgers University
New Brunswick, NJ 08903

NM　Bulletin Office
Dept. of Agricultural Information
Drawer 3A1
New Mexico State University
Las Cruces, NM 88001

NY　Mailing Room, Building 7
Research Park
Cornell University
Ithaca, NY 14850

NC　Publications Office
Dept. of Agriculture Info.
Box 5037—State College Station
North Carolina State Univ.
Raleigh, NC 27607

ND　Dept. of Agricultural Information
North Dakota State University
Fargo, ND 51802

OH　Extension Office
Ohio State University
2120 Fyffe Road
Columbus, OH 43210

OK　Central Mailing Services
Oklahoma State University
Stillwater, OK 74074

OR　Bulletin Mailing Service
Industrial Bldg.
Oregon State University
Corvallis, OR 97331

PA　Sales Supervisor
230 Agriculture Admin. Bldg.
Pennsylvania State University
University Park, PA 16802

RI　Resource Information Office
16 Woodward Hall
University of Rhode Island
Kingston, RI 02881

SC　Dept. of Agricultural Comm.
112 Plant and Animal Sci. Bldg.
Clemson University
Clemson, SC 29631

SD　Agricultural Information Office
Extension Building
South Dakota State University
Brookings, SD 57006

TN　Agricultural Ext. Service
Univ. of Tennessee
Box 1071
Knoxville, TN 37901

TX　Dept. of Agric. Communications
Texas A&M University
College Station, TX 77843

UT　Ext. Publications Officer
Library 124
Utah State University
Logan, UT 84321

VT　Publications Office
Morrill Hall
University of Vermont
Burlington, VT 05401

VA　Extension Division
Virginia Polytechnic Institute
Blacksburg, VA 24061

WA　Coop. Ext., Publications Bldg.
Washington State University
Pullman, WA 99163

WV　Coop. Ext. Service
West Virginia University
Morgantown, WV 26506

WI　Agricultural Bulletin Bldg.
1535 Observatory Drive
University of Wisconsin
Madison, WI 53706

WY　Bulletin Room, College of Agric.
University of Wyoming
Box 3354—University Station
Laramie, WY 82070

Mail-order rose suppliers

Burgess Seed and Plant Company (4)
Box 2000 Galesburg, MI 49053
This old, established nursery offers
some of the popular roses.

W. Atlee Burpee Company (5)
Warminster, PA 18974
Their large catalog includes a few
miniatures and shrub species, along
with favorite hybrid teas and climbers.

Jackson and Perkins (8)
Medford, OR 97501
"World's largest rose growers" offer
a 40-page catalog, mostly roses,
all modern.

**Farmer Seed and Nursery
Company** (9)
Faribault, MN 55021
Small selection of hybrid teas,
including subzeros, and floribundas.
A few shrubs and climbers.

**Henry Field Seed and Nursery
Company** (10)
Shenandoah, IA 51602
Miniatures and other modern classes,
including subzero hybrids.

**Gurney Seed and Nursery
Company** (12)
Yankton, SD 57078
Some old shrubs and the standard
modern roses.

**Earl May Seed and Nursery
Company** (18)
Shenandoah, IA 51603
Subzero roses and modern classifica-
tions; also products for growers.

Reuter Seed Company, Inc. (22)
320 N. Carrollton Avenue
New Orleans, LA 70119
A few popular rose varieties.

R. H. Shumway, Seedsman (26)
Rockford, IL 61101
Small collection of shrubs and
modern roses.

Armstrong Nurseries, Inc. (55)
Ontario, CA 91762
One of the major suppliers. Offers a
big colorful catalog of modern roses.

Arp Roses, Inc. (56)
P. O. Box 3338 Tyler, TX 75701
List of patented and nonpatented
popular roses.

Buckley Nursery Company (57)
Buckley, WA 98321
List of modern roses, including trees.

Carroll Gardens (58)
P. O. Box 310 444 East Main Street
Westminister, MD 22157
Collection of modern rose classes.

Eastern Roses (60)
Box 203
West Long Branch, NJ 07764
List of imported varieties for those with
the gambling spirit; small supply.

Roses By Fred Edmunds (61)
6235 S. West Kahle Road
Wilsonville, OR 97070
24-page catalog of modern roses.

Emlong's (62)
Stevensville, MI 49127
Small selection of modern roses,
including miniatures and shrubs.

Earl Ferris Nursery (63)
Hampton, IA 50441
Some shrubs and a collection of
modern roses.

Forrest Keeling Nursery (64)
Elsberry, MO 63343
Half a dozen hybrid teas and a
few shrubs.

Inter-State Nurseries (65)
Hamburg, IA 51644
Good collection of modern roses.

Kelly Brothers Nurseries, Inc. (66)
Dansville, NY 14437
A few shrub and species roses

Joseph J. Kern Rose Nursery (67)
Box 33
Mentor, OH 44060
No longer publishes a catalog. Grower
of unusual modern cultivars and many
old roses. Write for your request.

Kimbrew-Walter Rose Growers (68)
Route 1, Box 138-B
Wills Point, TX 75169
Good selection of modern classes.

Krider Nurseries, Inc. (69)
Middlebury, IN 46540
Modern roses, including subzeros, and
a few old-fashioned and shrub roses.

Kroh Brothers Nursery (70)
P.O. Box 536
Loveland, CO 80537
Selected old favorites and new cultivars.

Lamb Nurseries (71)
E. 101 Sharp Avenue
Spokane, WA 99202
Miniature roses included in their hardy
perennial catalog.

McDaniel's Miniature Roses (72)
7523 Zemco Street
Lemon Grove, CA 92045
List of miniature varieties.

Miniature Plant Kingdom (73)
4125 Harrison Grade Road
Sebastopol, CA 95472
Large selection of miniatures.

Mini-Roses (74)
P.O. Box 4255, Station A
Dallas, TX 75208
List of miniatures available.

**Moore Miniature Roses
(Sequoia Nursery)** (75)
2519 East Noble Avenue
Visalia, CA 93277
Large selection of miniature varieties.

Nor'east Miniature Roses (76)
58 Hammond Street
Rowley, MA 01969
List of miniatures.

Carl Pallek and Sons Nurseries (77)
Box 137
Virgil, Ontario, Canada L0S-1T0
List of popular and hard-to-find roses,
including some shrubs.

**'Pixie Treasures' Miniature
Rose Nursery** (78)
4121 Prospect Avenue
Yorba Linda, CA 92686
Large selection of miniature roses.

Port Stockton Nursery (79)
2910 East Main
Stockton, CA 95250
List of modern roses.

Roseway Nurseries (80)
2935 S. West 234th Avenue
Beaverton, OR 97005
Catalog of modern varieties.

Spring Hill Nurseries Company (81)
110 Elm Street
Tipp Ctiy, OH 45371
Small selection of hybrid teas, miniatures, and shrubs.

Stanek's Garden Center (82)
East 2929, 27th Avenue
Spokane, WA 99203
Modern cultivars, supplies, and a
few shrubs.

**Star Roses/The Conard-Pyle
Company** (83)
West Grove, PA 19390
Large catalog of modern roses, a few
shrubs, and products.

**Stark Brothers Nurseries and
Orchards Company** (84)
Louisiana, MO 63353
Small selection of modern roses
and shrubs.

Stern's Nurseries (85)
Geneva, NY 14456
Some shrubs, along with modern
classes, including subzero hybrids.

Stocking Rose Nursery (86)
785 North Capitol Avenue
San Jose, CA 95133
Modern cultivars, including miniatures,
and a few novelties.

P. O. Tate Nursery (87)
Route 3
Tyler, TX 75701
Old nursery offers popular modern
cultivars.

Taylor Nurseries (88)
4647 Union Bay Place NE
Seattle, WA 98105
Roses are their specialty, although
no current catalog is available. Write
your request for variety.

Tiny Petals Nursery
489 Minot
Chula Vista, CA 92010
Miniature roses.

Thomasville Nurseries, Inc. (89)
P. O. Box 7
Thomasville, GA 31792
A few old roses and a good selection
of modern ones.

Tillotson's Roses (90)
Brown's Valley Road
Watsonville, CA 95076
Roses of yesterday and some unusual
modern varieties.

**Percy H. Wright, (Moose Range
Gardens)** (91)
407 109th Street
Saskatoon, Saskatchewan, Canada
List of species and old roses. Will prop-
agate others with a year's notice.

**Melvin E. Wyant Rose Specialist,
Inc.** (92)
Johnny Cake Ridge, Route 84
Mentor, OH 44060
Both old-fashioned shrubs and modern
varieties, including miniatures.

McConnell Nursery Co., Ltd. (93)
Port Burwell, Ontario, Canada N0J-1T0
Modern roses, including some hard-to-
find ones and a few shrubs.

The nurseries on the opposite page offer lists of catalogs of retail roses. Write for those that offer the type of roses that interest you. It is not necessary to order from nearby nurseries, since the origin of the plant isn't as important as the quality.

Numbers following the company names are from Chevron Chemical Company's list of seed and nursery suppliers, and correspond to the source column on the charts beginning on page 28.

Buy plants cautiously

Rose plants are available either bareroot (wrapped and packaged, loose, or in plantable boxes) or growing in containers (often with full growth and even flowers). Either type plant will produce good roses. Container-grown bushes may give the gardener fewer problems at planting time, but the varieties available will not be as great.

Roses are graded by a rating system: 1, 1½, and 2—based on size and number of canes. If you're willing to pay the price for the best possible blooms, insist on Grade No. 1 plants with three or four heavy canes at least ⅜ inch in diameter; hybrid teas 18 inches in height and floribundas 15 inches. After a few seasons of growth, grade 1½ plants may catch up, but you miss those first years of good bloom quality. Inferior grades will not give you specimen flowers.

Purchase plants from well-known mail-order houses or licensed garden centers or nurseries. Buy from the people who sell roses year after year and stand behind the quality of their plants. Avoid bargains. You'll have a considerable investment of time and energy in each rose, so it's advisable to spend a little extra money you'd expect to pay for quality plants.

Most bareroot roses are grown in California where the environment produces top-grade plants that are just as hardy, (or perhaps more hardy), in cold climates as roses begun in northern fields.

The plants are harvested when they are dormant, held under ideal conditions, and shipped to retailers or directly to you at the right time for your local climatic conditions.

Bareroot roses held in dry, overheated stores for long periods cannot be expected to perform as well as a fresh plant that has been kept moist by a knowledgeable nurseryman or one sent directly from a mail-order supplier. Buy plants from retail stores only if the stock has been kept dormant and protected from drying.

Roses are grown in huge fields . . . dug from the soil . . . inspected, graded, pruned . . . labeled, and packaged for shipment.

Nurseries and garden centers offer bareroot roses or container-grown plants, often in bloom.

When you shop for plants, examine the rose bush to be sure the wood is not dry and shriveled. The plant should be well shaped, with no deformed growth, abnormal swellings, and discolorations on canes or roots, which may be symptoms of disease. Bark on the canes should be firm, plump, and green. The root system should be sturdy and fibrous, with several firm, well-branched roots.

How to read our rose charts

The following pages are intended to serve as guides in selecting roses we found available from commercial sources in the United States and Canada. This is certainly not a complete listing of what's available, but represents some of the most popular, easy-to-grow varieties, and a few forgotten or very new cultivars that deserve your attention.

Roses are divided by classification in order that you may locate them according to their basic growth habits. All spelling and information is based on listings of the American Rose Society.

The first column of the chart gives the name of the rose cultivar, species, sport, or variety, along with the year of its commercial introduction.

Column two gives the bloom color. Under flower description, you can locate the size, form (single, double, or semidouble), number of petals (to determine fullness), and the fragrance. Next is a brief description of the foliage and the growth habits of the plant.

The final column lists sources that offered the plant for sale at the time of publication. The numbers correspond to the catalog list on page 26. Suppliers change their stock regularly, so you may have to contact more than one source to find a particular rose you want.

Antigua

Apollo

Bewitched

Candy Stripe

Hybrid Teas

Rose and year of introduction	Color	Flower description	Foliage and growth habits	Catalog sources
American Heritage (1965)	Ivory and salmon	3-5″ Double (50-60 petals), no fragrance	Dark, leathery; tall, compact, moderate blooming	9, 59, 61, 65, 67, 69, 77, 83, 89, 92, 93
Antigua (1974)	Apricot blend	4½-6″ Double (25-30 petals), heavy, fruity-spicy fragrance	Bronzy, glossy, leathery; medium green; disease-resistant	8, 57, 77, 79, 80, 82, 92
Apollo (1971)	Medium yellow	5-6″ Double (30-35 petals), moderate to strong fragrance	Dark, glossy, leathery; disease-resistant, few thorns	10, 57, 58, 65, 69, 77, 79, 80, 83, 86, 87, 89, 92
Arctic Flame (1955)	Bright red	5″ Double (50-60 petals), moderate fragrance	Medium green; subzero plant, very vigorous	9, 12, 77, 85, 93
Beauté (1953)	Light orange	Large double, moderate fragrance	Vigorous, free-blooming	59, 67, 69, 77, 92
Bewitched (1967)	Rose Bengal	5″ Double (24-30 petals), spicy, old-fashioned fragrance	Glossy; easy to grow	61, 69, 77, 79, 80, 82, 86, 87, 89, 92, 93
Big Ben (1964)	Dark red	5-6″ Double, heavy fragrance	Dark; tall-growing	59, 60, 61, 67, 68, 77, 87, 92
Blanche Mallerin (1941)	Pure white	4″ Double (30-35 petals), moderate fragrance	Glossy, leathery; vigorous, few thorns	56, 67, 68, 69, 83, 87, 89, 92
Blue Moon (1964)	Lilac	4″ Double (40 petals), heavy fragrance	Medium green; very vigorous, free-blooming	59, 60, 61, 67, 77, 79, 92, 93
Candy Stripe (1963)	Dusty pink streaked lighter	6″ Double (60 petals), heavy, tea-rose fragrance	Dark, glossy; well-shaped plant	59, 77, 80, 83, 86, 93
Carla (1963)	Pink shaded salmon	3½-5″ Double (26 petals), moderate fragrance	Dark; vigorous, free-blooming	58, 59, 61, 68, 89, 92
Charlotte Armstrong (1940)	Red to cerise	3-4″ Double (35 petals), moderate tea-rose fragrance	Dark, leathery; very vigorous, compact, abundant bloom	5, 22, 55, 56, 57, 59, 61, 63
Chicago Peace (1962)	Pink and yellow	5-5½″ Double (50-60 petals), slight fragrance, good exhibition rose	Glossy, leathery; vigorous, upright, bushy	4, 5, 10, 22, 56, 57, 58, 59, 61, 65, 67, 68, 69, 70, 77, 80, 82, 83, 86, 87, 89, 92, 93
Christian Dior (1958)	Crimson flushed scarlet	4-4½″ Double (50-60 petals), slight fragrance	Dark, glossy, leathery; bushy plant, abundant blooms	59, 68, 69, 77, 79, 82, 83, 86, 87, 89, 92
Chrysler Imperial (1952)	Crimson-red	4½-5″ Double (40-50 petals), heavy fragrance	Dark; moderate-blooming	4, 5, 9, 10, 18, 22, 26, 55, 56, 57, 58, 59, 61, 62, 63, 64, 65, 67, 68, 69, 70, 77, 80, 81, 82, 83, 85, 86, 87, 89, 92, 93

Chrysler Imperial

Flaming Peace

Electron

Top: *Command Performance*
Bottom: *Double Delight*

Futura

Rose and year of introduction	Color	Flower description	Foliage and growth habits	Catalog sources
Command Performance (1970)	Orange-red	3-4" Semidouble (15-20 petals), heavy fragrance	Leathery; upright growth	5, 22, 57, 58, 59, 61, 62, 65, 69, 77, 80, 82, 87, 92, 93
Confidence (1951)	Light pink to yellow	Large double (28-38 petals), moderate fragrance	Dark, leathery; vigorous and bushy	4, 59, 61, 67, 68, 69, 83, 87, 89, 92
Crimson Glory (1935)	Deep crimson with purple	Large double (30 petals), heavy, old-fashioned fragrance	Leathery; spreading	5, 9, 12, 18, 22, 55, 56, 57, 59, 61, 63, 65, 67, 68, 69, 70, 77, 80, 82, 83, 85, 86, 87, 89, 90, 92
Dainty Bess (1925)	Rose-pink	3-4" Single (5 petals), moderate fragrance, good exhibition flower	Leathery; hardy plant	59, 61, 67, 79, 80, 82, 86, 89, 90, 92
Double Delight (1977)	Red and white	5½-6" Double (35-45 petals), heavy, spicy fragrance	Dark, glossy; spreading, quite bushy plant	5, 8, 55, 61, 68, 83, 86, 87, 89, 92, 93
Eclipse (1935)	Golden yellow	3-5" Double (25-30 petals), moderate fragrance	Leathery; tall, shapely plant	5, 26, 55, 56, 57, 59, 61, 63, 64, 65, 67, 69, 79, 80, 82, 83, 86, 87, 89, 92
Electron (1972)	Rose-pink	Large double, slight fragrance	Glossy, light green; some disease-resistance, free-blooming, many thorns	10, 22, 55, 57, 58, 59, 61, 62, 65, 68, 69, 77, 80, 82, 83, 86, 87, 89, 92
Etoile de Hollande (1919)	Bright red	Large double (35-45 petals), heavy, old-fashioned fragrance,	Medium green; moderate open growth	22, 56, 59, 86, 87
Firelight (1971)	Coral	6" Double, moderate fragrance	Leathery, light green; very vigorous, disease-resistant	8, 57, 58, 70, 77, 80, 82, 92
First Love (1951)	Rose to pink	2½-3½" Double (20-30 petals), slight fragrance	Leathery, light green; moderately bushy plant	59, 61, 67, 77, 80, 82, 86, 90
First Prize (1970)	Rose-pink with ivory	6" Double (25 petals), moderate fragrance, top U.S. exhibition rose	Dark, leathery; disease-resistant, upright, angular	4, 5, 8, 22, 55, 56, 57, 58, 59, 61, 62, 65, 67, 68, 70, 77, 79, 80, 82, 83, 86, 87, 89, 92
Flaming Peace (1965)	Crimson and yellow	Large double, moderate fragrance	Dark, glossy, leathery; abundant bloom	9, 18, 61, 65, 69, 70, 77, 80, 84, 92, 93
Forty-Niner (1949)	Cherry-red and yellow	3½-4" Double (25-40 petals), slight fragrance	Dark, glossy, leathery; compact, free-blooming	5, 10, 12, 55, 56, 65, 68, 69, 87
Fragrant Cloud (1968)	Coral-red	5" Double (25-30 petals), heavy, tea-rose fragrance, good show rose	Dark, glossy; very vigorous, very free-blooming	8, 55, 57, 58, 59, 61, 65, 68, 70, 77, 80, 82, 83, 86, 89, 90, 92
Fred Edmunds (1943)	Coppery orange	5-5½" Double (20-30 petals), heavy, spicy fragrance	Glossy, leathery; bushy, open	57, 61, 80, 86
Futura (1976)	Bright orange	4-5" Double, moderate fragrance, fewer petals in hot weather	Dark; very vigorous, compact	8, 57, 79, 80, 82, 86

Gypsy

Helen Traubel

Jadis

Medallion

Heirloom

Rose and year of introduction	Color	Flower description	Foliage and growth habits	Catalog sources
Garden Party (1959)	Pale yellow to white	4-5″ Double (25-30 petals), slight fragrance, often tinted light pink	Semiglossy; vigorous, bushy, well-branched	55, 59, 61, 65, 67, 68, 69, 77, 83, 84, 86, 87, 89, 92
Golden Gate (1972)	Yellow	5″ Double (30-35 petals), slight fragrance	Dark, glossy; abundant, continuous bloom	8, 57, 58, 68, 79, 80, 82, 86, 92
Golden Masterpiece (1954)	Golden yellow	Very large double (35 petals), moderate fragrance	Glossy; vigorous, upright	12, 22, 57, 59, 70, 77, 82, 84, 89, 92
Granada (1963)	Rose, red, and yellow	4-5″ Double (18-25 petals), moderate fragrance	Leathery, crinkled; vigorous, upright	58, 61, 67, 68, 69, 77, 80, 82, 83, 86, 87, 89
Gypsy (1972)	Orange-red	5″ Double (35-40 petals), slight, spicy fragrance	Glossy, leathery; above-average height	5, 10, 18, 56, 57, 58, 65, 69, 77, 79, 80, 82, 83, 86, 87, 89, 92
Heirloom (1972)	Deep lilac	4½″ Semidouble (35 petals), heavy fragrance	Dark, leathery; disease-resistant, profuse blooming	8, 58, 70, 77, 80, 82
Helen Traubel (1951)	Pink to apricot	5-6″ Double (20-25 petals), moderate fragrance, weak neck	Leathery, olive-green; tall, vigorous	5, 9, 10, 22, 58, 59, 61, 62, 65, 68, 69, 77, 80, 82, 83, 85, 86, 87, 89, 92
Irish Gold (1966)	Yellow	7″ Double (33 petals), moderate fragrance	Dark, glossy, leathery; upright, bushy plant	57, 58, 59, 61, 69, 80, 82, 86, 92
Jadis (1974)	Pink	4½″ Double; heavy, old-fashioned fragrance	Leathery, light green; disease-resistant, very prolific	8, 57, 77, 80, 82, 92
John F. Kennedy (1965)	White	5-6″ Double (45-50 petals), heavy fragrance, long-lasting	Leathery; very vigorous, profuse bloom	5, 8, 18, 22, 56, 57, 58, 59, 67, 69, 77, 82, 83, 86, 87, 89
Kaiserin Auguste Viktoria (1891)	Snowy white tinted lemon	Large double (100 petals), heavy fragrance	Dark; intermittent bloom	22, 56, 65, 68, 69, 70, 77, 87, 92
Katherine T. Marshall (1943)	Rose-pink flushed yellow	5″ Double (22 petals), light, spicy fragrance	Leathery; very vigorous, upright	12, 26, 56, 57, 65, 68, 69, 87
King's Ransom (1961)	Golden yellow	5-6″ Double (35-40 petals), moderate fragrance	Glossy, leathery; extremely long stems, not hardy	8, 56, 57, 59, 61, 65, 68, 69, 70, 77, 80, 82, 83, 86, 87, 92, 93
Kordes' Perfecta (1957)	Cream, crimson, and yellow	4½-5″ Double (65-70 petals), heavy, tea-rose fragrance, hot climate intensifies color	Dark, glossy, leathery	4, 5, 57, 58, 59, 61, 62, 67, 69, 77, 87, 92
Lady X (1966)	Mauve	Large double, slight fragrance	Leathery; vigorous, upright growth	58, 59, 61, 68, 77, 83, 86, 89, 92

Miss All-American
Beauty

Pascali

Percy Thrower

Perfume Delight

Rose and year of introduction	Color	Flower description	Foliage and growth habits	Catalog sources
Medallion (1973)	Apricot-buff	7-8″ Double (35 petals), moderate, fruity fragrance, good lasting quality	Leathery, light green; few thorns	5, 8, 10, 18, 26, 55, 56, 57, 58, 61, 62, 65, 68, 69, 70, 77, 80, 82, 83, 86, 87, 89, 92
Mirandy (1945)	Garnet-red	5-6″ Double (40-50 petals), heavy, old-fashioned fragrance	Leathery; bushy, compact	5, 22, 55, 56, 57, 58, 59, 62, 65, 67, 68, 69, 70, 77, 83, 84, 85, 87, 89, 92
Miss All-American Beauty (1965)	Dark pink	4-5″ Double (50-60 petals), heavy tea-rose fragrance, long-lasting blooms	Leathery; disease-resistant	55, 56, 57, 58, 59, 61, 65, 68, 69, 77, 79, 80, 82, 83, 86, 87, 89, 92, 93
Mister Lincoln (1964)	Dark red	4½-6″ Double (30-40 petals), heavy fragrance	Dark, leathery; moderate to free-blooming	4, 5, 55, 56, 57, 58, 59, 61, 62, 65, 67, 68, 69, 77, 79, 80, 82, 83, 84, 86, 87, 89, 92, 93
Mojave (1954)	Apricot-orange, tinted red	4-4½″ Double (25 petals), prominently veined, moderate fragrance	Glossy; vigorous, upright	10, 12, 18, 22, 55, 56, 58, 59, 61, 62, 63, 65, 67, 68, 69, 70, 77, 79, 80, 82, 85, 86, 87, 92
Oklahoma (1964)	Very dark red	4-5½″ Double (40-55 petals), heavy tea-rose fragrance	Dark, leathery; well-branched bushes	10, 55, 57, 58, 59, 61, 77, 80, 82, 83, 89, 92, 93
Oregold (1975)	Deep yellow	5″ Double (35-40 petals), slight fragrance, color does not fade	Dark, glossy; disease-resistant, vigorous, upright, bushy	4, 5, 8, 10, 18, 22, 26, 55, 56, 57, 58, 61, 62, 65, 68, 70, 77, 79, 80, 82, 83, 86, 87, 89, 92, 93
Papa Meilland (1963)	Dark crimson	Large double (35 petals), heavy fragrance	Glossy, leathery, olive-green; vigorous, upright growth	59, 60, 61, 67, 68, 77, 92, 93
Pascali (1963)	Creamy white	3-4″ Double (30 petals), slight fragrance, good exhibition rose	Dark; vigorous, bushy, very free-blooming	4, 55, 58, 59, 61, 67, 68, 70, 77, 80, 83, 84, 86, 87, 89, 92, 93
Peace (1945)	Yellow with rose-pink	6″ Double (40-45 petals), slight fragrance, voted world's favorite rose	Very dark, glossy, leathery; very vigorous, tall, bushy	4, 5, 8, 9, 10, 12, 18, 22, 55, 56, 57, 58, 59, 61, 62, 63, 64, 65, 67, 68, 69, 70, 77, 79, 80, 81, 82, 83, 84, 85, 86, 87, 89, 92, 93
Percy Thrower (1964)	Rose-pink	4-5″ Double (25-30 petals), moderate fragrance	Glossy; thrives in cool climates	60, 77, 79
Perfume Delight (1973)	Pink	Large double, heavy, spicy fragrance	Leathery; abundant, continuous bloom, upright, bushy	5, 10, 18, 22, 26, 55, 56, 57, 58, 61, 62, 65, 68, 69, 77, 79, 80, 82, 83, 86, 87, 89, 92
Peter Frankenfeld (1966)	Rose-pink	Large double, slight fragrance	Hardy, disease-resistant	59, 61, 67, 77, 92, 93

Portrait

Seashell   Smoky

Rose and year of introduction	Color	Flower description	Foliage and growth habits	Catalog sources
Picadilly (1960)	Scarlet and gold	4½-5" Double (25-30 petals), no fragrance	Dark, glossy; upright, branching	59, 61, 67, 69, 77, 80, 92
Pink Peace (1959)	Deep pink	4½-6" Double (50-60 petals), heavy fragrance	Leathery; tall-growing, well-branched	9, 18, 58, 59, 62, 65, 69, 77, 79, 80, 83, 87, 92, 93
Portrait (1971)	Pink	4" Double (35 petals), moderate fragrance, long-lasting	Dark, glossy, leathery; disease-resistant	10, 57, 61, 69, 77, 82, 83, 87, 89, 92
Promise (1976)	Light pink	5-6" Double (35-45 petals), slight fragrance	Glossy, medium green; abundant bloom	8, 57, 70, 79, 80
Proud Land (1969)	Deep red	4½-5½" Double (60 petals), moderate fragrance	Dark, leathery; very vigorous, upright growth	8, 57, 70, 77, 80, 82, 92
Queen o' the Lakes (1949)	Blood-red to carmine	Large double, moderate fragrance	Glossy; subzero plant, vigorous, bushy	9, 10, 18, 59, 77, 85
Red Devil (1970)	Light red	Large double (72 petals), moderate fragrance	Glossy, medium green; very vigorous	57, 59, 61, 68, 77, 80, 82, 86, 92
Red Masterpiece (1974)	Dark red	6" Double (35-40 petals), heavy fragrance	Dark, leathery; mildews, profuse blooming	4, 8, 57, 68, 77, 80, 82, 92
Red Radiance (1916)	Crimson	Medium double (23 petals), heavy, old-fashioned fragrance	Leathery; very vigorous, abundant bloom	22, 56, 65, 68, 89
Rose Gaujard (1957)	Cherry-red, pink, and white	3-4" Double (80 petals), slight fragrance	Glossy, leathery; free-blooming, bushy plant	59, 61, 77, 79, 80, 92
Royal Highness (1962)	Light pink	5-5½" Double (40-50 petals), heavy, tea-rose fragrance	Dark, glossy, leathery; upright, well-shaped plants	56, 59, 61, 65, 67, 77, 80, 82, 83, 84, 86, 87, 89, 92, 93
Rubaiyat (1946)	Rose-red	4½-5" Double (25 petals), heavy fragrance	Dark, leathery; quite hardy	59, 61, 65, 67, 69, 77, 92
Seashell (1976)	Peach-pink	4-5" Double (35-40 petals), heavy fragrance	Dark; abundant bloom on very ornamental bush	4, 5, 8, 10, 55, 56, 57, 61, 62, 65, 68, 70, 79, 80, 83, 86, 89
Smoky (1968)	Plum to orange-red	3½-4" Double (30-35 petals), slight fragrance, unusual ever-changing color	Light green; vigorous, upright	8, 10, 57, 62, 80
Snowfire (1973)	Scarlet and white	4-5" Double, slight fragrance	Dark, glossy; disease-resistant, many thorns	4, 8, 57, 68, 70, 77, 79, 80, 82, 86, 92
South Seas (1962)	Coral-pink	6-7" Double (45-50 petals), moderate fragrance	Leathery; vigorous, upright, prolific	57, 59, 61, 68, 77, 86, 87, 89, 92
Spellbinder (1975)	Ivory-pink-red	6" Double (25-30 petals), slight fragrance, good lasting quality	Dark, leathery; disease-resistant	8, 57, 77, 79, 80, 82, 92
Sterling Silver (1957)	Lilac	3½" Double (30 petals), heavy fragrance, open petals are grey in sunlight	Dark, glossy; vigorous, upright	5, 8, 9, 10, 18, 26, 55, 57, 58, 59, 65, 79, 80, 82, 86, 89

Spellbinder

Talisman

Tropicana

Rose and year of introduction	Color	Flower description	Foliage and growth habits	Catalog sources
Summer Sunshine (1962)	Deep yellow	3½-5" Double (25 petals), slight fragrance	Dark, leathery; well-branched, abundant bloom	55, 59, 61, 68, 69, 77, 79, 80, 82, 83, 86, 87, 92
Summerwine (1974)	Light rose-pink	4-6" Double (40-50 petals), no fragrance, clear, long-lasting color	Leathery; vigorous, very free-blooming	57, 70, 77, 79, 80
Sunset Jubilee (1973)	Medium pink	6" Double (40 petals), slight fragrance	Leathery, light green; abundant, continuous bloom	8, 57, 61, 77, 79, 80, 82, 86, 92
Sutter's Gold (1950)	Golden orange	4-5" Double (30-35 petals), heavy fragrance	Dark, leathery; very vigorous	5, 12, 22, 55, 58, 59, 61, 63, 65, 67, 69, 70, 77, 79, 80, 82, 85, 86, 89, 92, 93
Swarthmore (1963)	Rose-red	4" Double (45-55 petals), slight fragrance	Dark, leathery; very vigorous, bushy	59, 61, 67, 68, 77, 83, 86, 89, 92
Talisman (1929)	Yellow and copper	Medium double (25 petals), moderate fragrance, an old favorite bicolor	Glossy, leathery, light green; vigorous	5, 22, 56, 65, 69, 70, 79, 80, 83, 86, 87
Tallyho (1948)	Rose-red/ cardinal- red	3½-4" Double (35 petals), spicy fragrance	Leathery; unusually winter-hardy	59, 67, 69, 77, 92
The Doctor (1936)	Satiny pink	6" Double (25 petals), heavy fragrance, huge flowers worth waiting for	Light green; dwarf, bushy	5, 9, 10, 12, 18, 22, 65, 68, 87, 90
Tiffany (1954)	Rose to pink	4-5" Double (25-30 petals), heavy fragrance	Dark; very vigorous, upright	4, 55, 56, 57, 58, 59, 61, 62, 63, 64, 65, 67, 68, 69, 70, 77, 80, 81, 82, 83, 84, 86, 87, 89, 92
Tropicana (1960)	Coral- orange	5" Double (30-35 petals), heavy, fruity fragrance, colorfast	Dark, glossy, leathery; exceptionally vigorous	4, 5, 8, 9, 10, 18, 22, 26, 55, 56, 57, 58, 59, 61, 65, 67, 68, 69, 70, 77, 79, 80, 82, 83, 84, 86, 87, 89, 92, 93
V For Victory (1941)	Yellow tinted orange	Large Double (45 petals), heavy fragrance	Glossy; subzero plant, bushy	9, 12, 18, 77, 85, 93
Whisky Mac (1967)	Bronze- yellow	Large Double (28-30 petals), heavy fragrance	Glossy; very vigorous and bushy	59, 61, 77, 79, 92, 93
White Masterpiece (1969)	White	6" Double (60 petals), slight fragrance	Glossy; compact plant	8, 57, 58, 61, 68, 70, 77, 79, 80, 82, 86, 92
Yankee Doodle (1976)	Peach to apricot- yellow	5" Double (50 petals), slight, tea-rose fragrance	Dark, glossy; outstanding disease-resistance	4, 5, 8, 10, 26, 55, 56, 57, 61, 62, 65, 68, 70, 79, 80, 83, 86, 89, 93

Garden Party, a hybrid tea

Cathedral

Bon-Bon

Garnette

Floribundas & Polyanthas

Rose and year of introduction	Color	Flower description	Foliage and growth habits	Catalog sources
Angel Face (1968)	Lavender edged red	4″ Double (30-40 petals), heavy, old-fashioned fragrance, good exhibition rose	Dark, leathery; vigorous, upright, bushy	8, 10, 18, 22, 55, 56, 58, 59, 61, 62, 65, 68, 69, 77, 80, 82, 83, 86, 87, 89, 92, 93
Apricot Nectar (1965)	Pink-apricot, golden base	4-4½″ Double (35-40 petals), fruity fragrance	Dark, glossy; good in hot areas, very disease-resistant	8, 57, 59, 61, 80, 89, 92
Bahia (1974)	Orange	4″ Double (20-30 petals), spicy fragrance	Bronzy, glossy; vigorous, hardy	10, 55, 57, 58, 61, 62, 65, 77, 79, 82, 83, 86, 89, 92
Betty Prior (1935)	Carmine-pink	2-3″ Single (5 petals), moderate fragrance	Dark; hardy, disease-resistant	9, 57, 58, 59, 63, 65, 67, 68, 69, 80, 82, 83, 87, 92
Bon-Bon (1974)	Deep rose-white	3½″ Double (25 petals), moderate fragrance	Glossy, grey-green; very prolific bloomer	8, 10, 18, 55, 58, 61, 68, 77, 80, 82, 83, 86, 87, 89, 92
Cathedral (1976)	Apricot to salmon	3-3½″ Double (15 petals), heavy fragrance	Glossy, olive-green; highly mildew-resistant	8, 10, 22, 55, 56, 57, 61, 62, 65, 68, 79, 80, 83, 86, 89
Cécile Brunner (1881)*	Bright pink/yellow	1-1½″ Double, moderate fragrance, the "sweetheart" rose	Dark; slow-growing	57, 68, 71, 79, 80, 82, 86, 87, 89, 92
China Doll (1946)*	Rose-pink/yellow	1-2″ Double (20-26 petals), slight fragrance	Leathery; extremely profuse	55, 68, 69, 77, 79, 80, 86, 87, 89
Circus (1956)	Yellow, pink-salmon, and scarlet	2½-3″ Double (45-58 petals), spicy tea fragrance	Leathery, semiglossy; compact and bushy	10, 26, 55, 57, 59, 65, 77, 79, 80, 82, 83, 86, 87, 93
Europeana (1963)	Dark crimson	3″ Double (25-30 petals), slight fragrance, top-rated exhibition floribunda	Bronze-green; very free-blooming	4, 10, 18, 55, 56, 57, 58, 59, 61, 65, 68, 69, 77, 79, 80, 82, 83, 86, 87, 89, 92, 93
Eutin (1940)	Carmine-red	2-3″ Double, slight fragrance	Dark, glossy, leathery; robust, disease-resistant	9, 10, 12, 18, 26, 59, 63, 65, 68, 69, 77, 84, 85, 87, 89
Fashion (1949)	Deep peach	3-3½″ Double (21-25 petals), moderate fragrance	Bronzy; disease-resistant, spreading	12, 18, 22, 26, 56, 57, 59, 63, 65, 67, 68, 69, 77, 80, 82, 83, 84, 85, 87, 89, 92, 93
First Edition (1977)	Coral	2½″ Double, slight fragrance, color deepens in cool climate	Glossy, light green	5, 8, 55, 61, 68, 83, 86, 87, 89, 92, 93
Frensham (1946)	Deep scarlet	2-3″ Semidouble (15 petals), slight fragrance	Glossy; abundant, very free-blooming	9, 12, 59, 61, 63, 65, 67, 80, 90, 92

Orangeade

The Fairy

Redgold

Rose and year of introduction	Color	Flower description	Foliage and growth habits	Catalog sources
Garnette (1951)	Garnet-red/yellow	1-2″ Double (50 petals), slight fragrance, long-lasting flowers	Dark, leathery; susceptible to mildew	9, 18, 68, 80, 82, 89, 90
Gene Boerner (1968)	Deep pink	3½″ Double (35 petals), slight fragrance	Glossy; vigorous, upright	8, 55, 57, 58, 59, 61, 65, 77, 80, 82, 83, 86, 87, 92
Iceberg (1958)	White	2½-4″ Double, heavy fragrance	Glossy, light green; very disease-resistant	10, 58, 59, 61, 65, 67, 68, 69, 77, 79, 80, 86, 90, 92
Ivory Fashion (1958)	Ivory white	4-4½″ Semidouble (15-18 petals), moderate fragrance	Leathery; vigorous, upright	59, 61, 68, 77, 86, 90, 92
Jiminy Cricket (1954)	Coral-orange to pink-coral	3-4″ Double (25-30 petals), moderate fragrance like rose geranium	Glossy; bushy	57, 59, 65, 80, 82, 87
Little Darling (1956)	Yellow to salmon-pink	2½″ Double (24-30 petals), spicy fragrance	Dark, glossy, leathery; very vigorous	57, 59, 61, 67, 68, 69, 77, 80, 82, 86, 92
Margo Koster (1931)*	Salmon	1-2″ Double, slight fragrance, clusters	Glossy; often sold as florist pot plant	67, 68, 79, 80, 86, 87, 89
Orangeade (1959)	Bright orange	2½″ Semidouble (7 petals), slight fragrance, long-lasting	Dark; vigorous, bushy	61, 67, 77, 79, 92
Picnic (1976)	Coral-orange	4″ Double (25 petals), slight fragrance	Glossy; exceedingly free-blooming	8, 57, 80
Redgold (1971)	Gold edged pink	2-3″ Double (25-30 petals), slight fragrance, very long-lasting	Light green	8, 22, 55, 57, 58, 59, 61, 62, 65, 68, 69, 70, 77, 80, 82, 83, 86, 87, 89, 92
Red Pinocchio (1947)	Carmine-red	3″ Double (25-30 petals), moderate fragrance	Dark, leathery; tall and spreading in warmer climates	18, 22, 56, 57, 59, 62, 63, 65, 67, 68, 69, 70, 77, 84, 87, 89
Rose Parade (1975)	Coral-pink	2½″ Double (25-30 petals), heavy fragrance	Dark; profuse blooms	5, 8, 10, 18, 22, 55, 56, 57, 58, 61, 62, 65, 68, 69, 70, 80, 82, 83, 86, 87, 89, 92
Saratoga (1963)	White	4″ Double (30-35 petals), heavy fragrance, irregular clusters	Glossy, leathery; vigorous, upright, bushy	10, 58, 77, 80, 82, 83, 86, 92
Spartan (1955)	Orange-red	3-3½″ Double (30 petals), heavy fragrance	Dark, glossy, leathery; disease-resistant	10, 18, 56, 57, 58, 59, 63, 65, 68, 69, 70, 77, 83, 86, 87, 89, 92
The Fairy (1941)*	Pink	1-1½″ Double, no fragrance	Glossy; compact, hardy, spreading	10, 58, 59, 61, 63, 65, 67, 68, 69, 80, 83, 85, 86, 89, 90, 92
Vogue (1951)	Cherry-coral	3½-4½″ Double (25 petals), moderate fragrance	Glossy; vigorous, upright, bushy	59, 65, 68, 69, 70, 82
Woburn Abbey (1962)	Salmon-orange	3½″ Double (25 petals), moderate fragrance	Dark, leathery; moderate growth, free-blooming	57, 59, 77, 82, 92

*Polyantha

Aquarius

Prominent

Olé

Cherry-Vanilla

Sunsong

Grandifloras

Rose and year of introduction	Color	Flower description	Foliage and growth habits	Catalog sources
Aquarius (1971)	Pink	4″ Double (30-35 petals), moderately fragrant, long-lasting	Leathery, large; disease-resistant; upright, bushy	55, 57, 58, 61, 65, 68, 69, 77, 80, 86, 87, 92
Arizona (1975)	Golden copper	4½″ Double, moderately fragrant	Dark, semiglossy; tall plant	5, 8, 10, 18, 22, 55, 56, 57, 58, 61, 62, 65, 68, 69, 70, 79, 80, 82, 83, 86, 87, 89, 93
Camelot (1964)	Salmon	3½-4″ Double (40-55 petals), spicy fragrance	Glossy, leathery; moderate blooming	56, 58, 59, 61, 69, 77, 79, 82, 83, 86, 87, 92
Carrousel (1950)	Dark red	3-4″ Semidouble (20 petals), moderately fragrant	Dark, leathery; among the tallest of roses	55, 59, 77, 82, 84, 92
Cherry-Vanilla (1973)	Soft yellow to deep pink	Medium double, moderate tea fragrance	Dark, leathery, semiglossy; very vigorous, upright	55, 68, 79
Comanche (1968)	Red-orange	3½-4½″ Double, slight fragrance	Leathery; very vigorous, bushy; quick repeat bloomer	22, 56, 57, 59, 65, 69, 77, 79, 83, 86, 87
Hocus-Pocus (1976)	Orange-red, maroon	4½″ Double (25-35 petals), slight tea fragrance	Dense, dark, large, semiglossy; medium height; very floriferous	55, 68, 79
Montezuma (1955)	Orange-red	3½-4″ Double (32-40 petals), slight fragrance	Leathery, semiglossy; very vigorous, compact	10, 55, 56, 58, 59, 61, 65, 68, 69, 70, 77, 79, 82, 83, 86, 87, 89
Mount Shasta (1963)	White	4½-5″ Double (20-26 petals), moderate fragrance	Grey-green, leathery; good for cool climates	10, 59, 61, 67, 68, 77, 82, 86, 89, 92, 93
Olé (1964)	Orange-red	Medium double (45-55 petals), moderate fragrance	Glossy; vigorous and prolific	55, 61, 62, 68, 77, 80, 82, 86, 89
Prominent (1977)	Hot orange shaded yellow	3″ Double, slight fragrance, nonfading	Dark; disease-resistant	5, 8, 55, 61, 68, 83, 86, 87, 89, 92, 93
Queen Elizabeth (1954)	Carmine-rose to dawn-pink	3½-4″ Double (37-40 petals), moderate fragrance	Dark, glossy, leathery; the top-rated Grandiflora	9, 10, 18, 22, 55, 57, 58, 59, 61, 62, 63, 65, 68, 69, 70, 77, 79, 80, 81, 82, 83, 85, 86, 87, 89, 92, 93
Scarlet Knight (1966)	Crimson-scarlet	4-5″ Double, slight fragrance	Leathery; disease-resistant	18, 56, 58, 68, 69, 70, 77, 79, 82, 83, 86, 87, 89, 92, 93
Sonia (1975)	Coral-pink	4″ Double, spicy fragrance	Light green; profuse bloom	58, 65, 69, 70, 79, 80, 82, 83, 86, 89, 92
Sunsong (1976)	Orange to coral	3¼″ Double (55-70 petals), slight tea fragrance	Glossy; profuse bloom	55, 79

Redgold, floribunda

Fire Chief, miniature

Blaze, climbing

Fragrant Cloud, hybrid tea

Select elegant standards or tree roses

These stately plants are not a class of roses at all, but they are considered a distinct garden form. Almost any of the hybrid teas, floribundas, grandifloras, or miniatures listed in these pages can be grown as tree roses, or standards. Nurserymen simply graft the selected cultivar onto a tall trunk of established rootstock to create this elegant form. The flower and foliage characteristics remain the same as those of the grafted cultivars described in these charts.

In lieu of a chart listing tree roses available at publication, which would soon be outdated, here's a list of growers who will ship trees. Availability is variable from year to year. Check current catalogs for current offerings. In some cases, nurseries will even graft a tree rose especially for you, if you're willing to wait a year or two for the order.

Standards lend themselves to a variety of landscape uses and are a must for traditional or formal garden design. They usually need special winter protection (see page 61) and careful pruning (see page 59).

Tree rose sources: Armstrong Nurseries, Buckley Nursery, Earl May Seed, Emlong's, Gurney Seed, Inter-State Nurseries, Jackson and Perkins, McConnel Nursery, McDaniel's Miniature Roses, Melvin E. Wyant, Rose Specialist, Moore Miniature Roses, 'Pixie Treasures' Miniature Rose Nursery, Roseway Nurseries, Stanek's Garden Center, Stocking Rose Nursery, Thomasville Nurseries. (See page 26 for addresses.)

America

Don Juan

Tropicana, climbing

Climbers

Rose and year of introduction	Color	Flower description	Foliage and growth habits	Catalog sources
America (1976)	Coral-pink	4-5″ Double, spicy fragrance	Dark, leathery; Large-flowered Climber; profuse bloom	4, 5, 8, 10, 55, 56, 57, 61, 62, 65, 68, 70, 79, 80, 83, 86, 89
Blaze (1932)	Scarlet	2-3″ Semidouble (20 petals), slight fragrance	Dark, leathery; Large-flowered Climber; easy to grow, thrives everywhere	4, 5, 8, 9, 10, 18, 26, 55, 56, 57, 58, 62, 63, 64, 65, 67, 68, 69, 70, 77, 79, 80, 81, 82, 83, 84, 85, 86, 87, 89, 92, 93
Blossomtime (1951)	Pink	4″ Double (35-40 petals), heavy fragrance	Dark; Large-flowered Climber; low-growing (6 to 7′)	10, 58, 59, 67, 69, 77, 82, 83, 89, 90, 92
City of York (1945)	Creamy white	Large semidouble (15 petals), moderate fragrance	Glossy, leathery; Large-flowered Climber; profuse bloom	59, 67
Coral Dawn (1952)	Rose-pink	5″ Double (30-35 petals), moderate fragrance	Leathery; Large-flowered Climber; vigorous, 8-12′	55, 57, 59, 70, 77, 82, 83, 93
Coral Satin (1960)	Coral	3½-4″ Double (25 petals), moderate fragrance	Glossy, leathery; Large-flowered Climber; free-blooming, 6-8′	59, 77, 92
Crimson Glory, climbing (1946)	Deep crimson to purple	3-4½″ Double (30 petals), heavy, spicy fragrance	Leathery; Climbing Hybrid Tea; fast-growing	5, 9, 18, 55, 56, 57, 58, 62, 68, 69, 83, 84, 87, 89, 90
Don Juan (1958)	Dark red	5″ Double (35 petals), heavy fragrance, fade-resistant, good cutting	Dark, glossy, leathery; Large-flowered Climber	5, 8, 10, 18, 55, 56, 57, 59, 61, 65, 68, 69, 77, 80, 82, 83, 86, 87, 89, 92
Dortmund (1955)	Strawberry-red	2½-3½″ Single (5-7 petals), moderate fragrance	Glossy, light green; Kordesii shrub; very vigorous, profuse bloom	61, 90
Doctor J. H. Nicolas (1940)	Rose-pink	5″ Double (50 petals), moderate fragrance	Dark, leathery; Large-flowered Climber; recurrent bloom	9, 58, 59, 62, 63, 65, 80, 85, 92
Golden Showers (1956)	Daffodil-yellow	4″ Double (20-35 petals), moderate fragrance	Dark, glossy; Large-flowered Climber; long, almost thornless stems	4, 5, 8, 9, 10, 18, 26, 55, 56, 57, 58, 59, 61, 65, 68, 69, 77, 80, 83, 87, 89, 92, 93
Gold Rush (1941)	Gold	Large Double (24 petals), moderate fragrance	Glossy; Large-flowered Climber, not dependably recurrent	9, 12, 18, 58, 63, 65, 90
Handel (1965)	Rose-pink edged cream	3½″ Double (22 petals), no fragrance	Glossy, olive-green; Large-flowered Climber; free-growing, recurrent	61, 67, 77, 80

Handel

Joseph's
Coat

Rose and year of introduction	Color	Flower description	Foliage and growth habits	Catalog sources
Heidelberg (1959)	Bright to light crimson	4" Double (52 petals), no fragrance	Glossy, leathery; Kordesii shrub; very vigorous, profuse bloom	59, 77, 90
High Noon, climbing (1946)	Yellow tinted red	3-4" Double (25-30 petals), spicy fragrance	Glossy, leathery; Climbing Hybrid Tea; vigorous, to 8', recurrent	55, 68, 69, 80, 85, 86
Joseph's Coat (1964)	Yellow and red	3" Double, slight fragrance	Dark, glossy; Large-flowered Climber; very free-blooming	9, 10, 18, 55, 61, 63, 65, 68, 70, 80, 86, 89
New Dawn (1930)	Pink	2-3" Double, slight fragrance	Dark, glossy; Large-flowered Climber; continuous blooming, to 20'	26, 55, 59, 67, 69, 83, 89
Paul's Scarlet Climber (1916)	Scarlet	2-3" Semidouble (20 petals), slight fragrance	Dark; Large-flowered Climber; very hardy and profuse	9, 10, 12, 18, 26, 57, 63, 65, 69, 70, 79, 81
Peace, climbing (1950)	Yellow edged pink	4-5½" Double (40-45 petals), slight fragrance	Dark, glossy, leathery; Climbing Hybrid Tea; shy bloom until established, 15-20'	5, 10, 18, 55, 56, 57, 58, 79, 83, 84, 86, 87, 89, 92
Red Fountain (1975)	Dark red	3" Double, heavy, old-fashioned fragrance	Dark, leathery; Large-flowered Climber; disease-resistant, 10-12'	68, 69, 83, 92, 93
Rhonda (1968)	Carmine-rose	3-4" Double (40 petals), slight fragrance	Dark, glossy; Large-flowered Climber; defies bad weather and pests	5, 58, 61, 68, 77, 79, 83, 86, 92, 93
Royal Gold (1957)	Golden yellow	4" Double (30-40 petals), fruity fragrance	Glossy; Large-flowered Climber; vigorous pillar	8, 57, 59, 70, 77, 80, 82, 86, 89, 92
Show Garden, climbing (1954)	Crimson to rose and magenta	4-5" Double (40-45 petals), no fragrance	Large-flowered Climber; free-blooming	10, 12, 18, 59, 63, 65
Talisman, climbing (1930)	Yellow and copper	Medium double (25 petals), moderate fragrance	Glossy, light green; Climbing Hybrid Tea, vigorous plant	55, 62, 79, 86, 87, 89
Tropicana, climbing (1971)	Coral-orange	5" Double (30-35 petals), heavy, fruity fragrance	Dark, glossy; Climbing Hybrid Tea; strong stems produce many blooms	18, 55, 57, 68, 80, 89, 92
Viking Queen (1963)	Medium to deep pink	3-4" Double (60 petals), heavy fragrance	Dark, glossy, leathery; Large-flowered Climber; profuse, recurrent bloom	9, 12, 59, 67, 92
White Dawn (1949)	White	2-3" Double (35 petals), moderate fragrance, gardenialike blooms	Glossy; Large-flowered Climber	4, 9, 10, 12, 18, 55, 57, 58, 63, 65, 77, 80, 82, 83, 92

Beauty
Secret

Green Ice

Janna

Baby
Darling

Gold Coin

Judy
Fischer

Miniatures

Rose and year of introduction	Color	Flower description	Foliage and growth habits	Catalog sources
Baby Darling (1964)	Orange to orange-pink	1-1½" Double (20 petals), no fragrance	Medium green; bushy growth	58, 71, 72, 73, 74, 75, 78, 86, 92
Baby Gold Star (1940)	Golden yellow	1½-2" Semidouble (12-15 petals), slight fragrance	Medium green; rather large plant	5, 10, 58, 72, 73, 74, 75, 76, 78, 83
Beauty Secret (1965)	Cardinal-red	1-1½" Double, heavy fragrance	Glossy, leathery; abundant bloom	5, 62, 71, 72, 73, 74, 75, 76, 78, 81, 82, 86, 92
Chipper (1966)	Salmon-pink	½-1" Double, slight fragrance	Glossy, leathery; vigorous growth	58, 72, 73, 74, 75, 76, 78, 83, 92
Cricri (1958)	Salmon shaded coral	2" Double (100 petals), no fragrance	Leathery; very bushy, profuse bloom	5, 62, 67, 71, 72, 73, 74, 75, 78, 81, 92
Debbie (1966)	Yellow edged pink	1½" Double, moderate fragrance	Leathery; sometimes semiclimbing	71, 72, 73, 74, 75, 78, 92
Fire Princess (1969)	Orange-red	1¾" Double, no fragrance	Glossy, leathery; vigorous, bushy	58, 72, 73, 74, 75, 76, 93
Gold Coin (1967)	Buttercup-yellow	Small double, moderate fragrance	Dark, leathery; very free bloom	5, 58, 72, 73, 74, 75, 76, 78, 81, 82, 83, 92
Golden Angel (1975)	Deep yellow	Medium double (60 to 70 petals), sweet fragrance, extra long-lasting cut	Dull green; rounded to spreading	72, 73, 75, 76, 78, 86, 92
Green Ice (1971)	White to green	1½" Double, no fragrance, pink buds	Glossy, leathery, medium green; disease-resistant	12, 72, 73, 74, 75, 78, 81, 82, 93
Hi Ho (1964)	Light red	Small double, no fragrance	Glossy; vigorous, climbing habit	72, 73, 75, 76, 78, 92
Janna (1970)	Pink, white	1½" Double, no fragrance, long-lasting	Leathery, medium green	72, 73, 74, 75, 76, 78, 82, 92
Jet Trail (1964)	White	Small double (35-45 petals), no fragrance	Medium green; bushy	71, 72, 73, 74, 75, 76, 78
Judy Fischer (1968)	Rose-pink	1½" Double, no fragrance	Bronzy, dark, leathery; low-growing, bushy	71, 72, 73, 74, 75, 76, 78, 82, 86, 92, 93
June Time (1963)	Light pink to dark pink	Small double (75 petals), no fragrance	Glossy; bushy and compact, abundant blooming	12, 58, 73, 74, 75, 78
Kara (1972)	Pink	¾" Single, no fragrance, long-lasting	Medium green; disease-resistant	58, 72, 73, 74, 75, 76, 78
Lavender Lace (1968)	Lavender	1½" Double, moderate fragrance	Glossy; vigorous and bushy	12, 58, 62, 71, 72, 73, 74, 75, 76, 78, 81, 82, 92

Lavender Lace

Over the Rainbow

Small World

My Valentine

Stacey Sue

Rose and year of introduction	Color	Flower description	Foliage and growth habits	Catalog sources
Little Curt (1971)	Deep red	1¾″ Semidouble to double, no fragrance	Dark, leathery; continuous bloom, disease-resistant	12, 72, 73, 74, 75, 76, 78
Mary Adair (1966)	Apricot	1¾″ Double, moderate fragrance	Light green; compact	72, 73, 74, 76, 78, 82
Mary Marshall (1970)	Orange-red, yellow base	1¾″ Double, moderate fragrance	Leathery, medium green; disease-resistant, continuous bloom	12, 58, 72, 73, 74, 75, 76, 78, 86, 92
Max Colwell (1975)	Red	1½″ Double (20-30 petals), slight fragrance	Leathery, medium green; spreading	72, 73, 74, 75, 76, 78, 82, 92
My Valentine (1975)	Red	1¼″ Double, no fragrance	Bronzy, glossy; rounded habit, good for pots	72, 73, 74, 75, 76, 78, 86, 92
Over the Rainbow (1974)	Red and yellow	1¾″ Double, slight fragrance	Leathery, medium green; abundant, continuous bloom	58, 72, 73, 74, 75, 76, 78, 82, 92
Persian Princess (1970)	Coral-red	2″ Double, moderate fragrance, long-lasting	Leathery, medium green	72, 73, 74, 75, 76, 78, 82
Pink Mandy (1974)	Pink	1″ Double (40 petals), no fragrance	Glossy, leathery; low-growing, disease-resistant	72, 73, 74, 75, 76, 78, 82
Shooting Star (1972)	Yellow tipped red	1″ Semidouble, slight fragrance	Light green; disease-resistant	72, 73, 74, 76, 78, 81, 83, 92
Small World (1975)	Orange-red	¾″ Semidouble (20-22 petals), no fragrance	Glossy, medium green; very compact and rounded	72, 73, 74, 75, 76
Stacey Sue (1976)	Pink	1″ Double, no fragrance	Glossy; very bushy	75, 76
Starina (1965)	Orange-scarlet	1½-2″ Double, no fragrance, top-rated U.S. rose	Glossy; vigorous, abundant blooming	58, 72, 73, 74, 75, 76, 78, 81, 82, 83, 86, 92
Sweet Fairy (1946)	Apple-blossom pink	¾-1″ Double (50-65 petals), moderate fragrance	Dark; moderately compact	5, 26, 58, 72, 73, 76, 78
Toy Clown (1966)	White edged red	1½″ Semidouble (20 petals), no fragrance	Leathery; bushy	5, 62, 71, 72, 73, 74, 75, 76, 78, 81, 82, 86, 92
White Angel (1971)	White	1¼″ Double, slight fragrance, good exhibition rose	Light green; bushy, profuse blooms	58, 72, 73, 74, 75, 76, 78, 82, 86, 92
Windy City (1974)	Pink	1½″ Double, slight fragrance, long-lasting	Bronzy; disease-resistant	72, 73, 74, 75, 76, 78, 92
Yellow Doll (1962)	Yellow to cream	1½″ Double (50-60 petals), moderate fragrance, good show rose	Glossy, leathery; vigorous, bushy	12, 62, 72, 73, 74, 75, 76, 78, 81, 86, 92
Yellow Jewel (1973)	Yellow	1½″ Semidouble (10 petals), moderate fragrance	Glossy, leathery; bushy, continuous bloom	58, 72, 73, 74, 75, 76, 78, 82, 93

There's more than one way to grow a rose

If you talk to rosarians, read articles on rose culture, check recommendations from state universities, and consult several commercial rose growers' guides, one fact will become evident: *There is more than one way to grow a rose.*

In this section you'll find a summary of our research into gardening practices of people who grow roses successfully. Most of the people we talked to, and listened to, realize that other quite successful methods may differ, but they still feel their way is the best. It's like raising a good crop of vegetables or having a house full of lush greenery. You must find your own way through experience—and even a few failures—to a program of rose culture that works best for you.

Roses have a built-in determination to live. This "will-to-grow" accounts for their growing wild in all temperate regions, under a great variety of soil and climatic conditions. They survive all the summer heat, high humidity, dry air, cool fog, strong winds, rains, and countless other abuses nature may hurl their way. They'll even take quite a lot of abuse from unsympathetic gardeners. But couple their built-in will-to-grow with proper care from an attentive gardener, and the rewards will be beautiful.

◁

Three gardeners prove our point that there's more than one way to grow a rose. Top photo shows traditional tramping of soil around a newly planted bareroot bush. In the lower left a pick handle is used to compact soil around a transplanted container-grown rose. In the lower right air pockets in container soil are eliminated by hand.

A rose bush with a full quota of clean leaves, and with a constant supply of moisture and nutrients will produce more than twice the blooms of one that is scantily fed and partially protected from pests, diseases, and the elements.

Class them easy to grow, and economical, too

A lot of people put down roses as too tricky and too time-consuming for the average gardener. It is certainly true that it takes some effort to grow *good* roses, just like it takes effort to grow *good* tomatoes or marigolds. But a healthy plant will continue to produce generous quantities of blooms! It could be that you'll find growing roses a lot easier than planting annuals or bulbs year after year.

It may be a job to water, feed, and protect roses from insects and disease, but look on it as a weekly visit with your roses. Then these tasks will be pleasant experiences. Think positively and class roses as easy to grow.

The initial cost of planting roses may seem to be greater than it is for seed or bedding plants. But compare the cost and labor of continually replacing annuals and bulbs with the number of rose blooms produced spring through fall, year after year, and you'll see that roses compensate in every way for the money you invest in them.

Selecting a site

Roses perform best when they receive full sunshine all day. If this is not possible, they should be planted where they will get a minimum of six hours direct sunlight daily. Morning sun is essential; partial afternoon shade is acceptable.

There should be air movement through the foliage to keep it dry and discourage diseases. Plant the bushes away from large trees or shrub masses which compete for nutrients, moisture, and sunlight.

Drainage is a critical factor for roses. If the desired site doesn't drain well, there are several ways to modify the area.

Some people add several inches of a loose medium such as volcanic cinder or gravel below the bottom level of the prepared soil. Excess water will drain into this loose medium.

You can dig a large trench beneath the planting site, and bury a drain tile or pipe in coarse gravel. Drain openings should be covered with asphalt roofing paper to prevent soil from washing in and clogging the holes. The pipe should be slightly slanted toward a ditch, storm sewer, or dry well.

An easier solution is to build a raised bed. In very moist areas build up a bed at least 10 to 15 inches. The side construction can be redwood or masonry framing, old railway ties, even stone or brick. In addition to giving excellent drainage, you'll find raised beds a pleasant way to do all the gardening chores. A seat cap lets you sit down beside the roses to work.

Consider possible erosion problems before planting on a hillside or slope. Terracing can solve your problem. This is merely a modified raised-bed approach. See the illustration below for details.

Roses do well in a wide range of soils, but prefer loamy soil with high humus content, at least two feet deep. A recipe for an ideal growing medium is:

5 parts (by volume) loamy soil
4 parts organic matter, such as compost or leaf mold, dehydrated cow manure, peat moss, or shredded bark (all available from garden centers)
1 part builder's sand

If you use manure, add 3 to 4 pounds of nourishing superphosphate

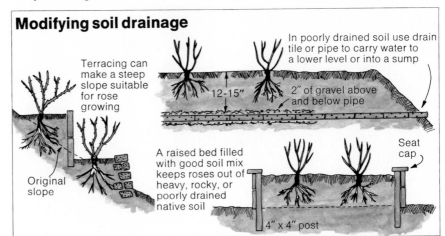

Modifying soil drainage

Terracing can make a steep slope suitable for rose growing

Original slope

In poorly drained soil use drain tile or pipe to carry water to a lower level or into a sump

12-15"

2" of gravel above and below pipe

A raised bed filled with good soil mix keeps roses out of heavy, rocky, or poorly drained native soil

Seat cap

4" x 4" post

per 100 square feet of soil surface for stronger root development.

If you're planting bushes individually, and the soil is good, dig holes 14 to 16 inches wide, and 12 to 15 inches deep. Work organic matter and sand into the dug-out soil. Use the same principle for a large bed of roses. Most experts advise preparing the soil area three to six months prior to planting the roses.

In cases of extremely poor soil, it may be necessary to remove all existing soil to a depth of 12 to 15 inches and totally replace it with a mixture of good loam, sand, and organic matter.

Roses respond best in a slightly acid soil with a pH of 6.0 to 6.5. Make a soil test to determine the acidity. If the soil is on the alkaline side, add agricultural sulfur at the rate of 2 pounds per 100 square feet and work into the soil.

Preplanting fumigation is a good idea if there's a history of nematodes or some soil-borne disease, or if the area has a large weed population. The most satisfactory fumigant for roses is methyl bromide, a gas released under an airtight cover. Your County Extension Agent can provide more information and recommend nearby professional help to apply the fumigant.

When you plant a rose

Start with strong-rooted, healthy plants with plump, fresh-looking canes. See page 27 for tips on buying rose bushes.

Planting times for packaged or bareroot roses:

Coldest winter temperature	Planting time
10° F.	Anytime bushes are dormant
—10° F.	Fall or spring
Below —10° F.	Spring only

Container-grown roses can be transplanted into the garden at any time from spring to fall.

If you're planting in the winter or early spring, get bareroot plants into the ground as early as weather will permit. Early planting gives roots a chance to start growth before the tops break into leaf.

By the time you receive your roses there's probably been some drying out in storage and shipping. To insure a good start, either bury roots and tops in wet peat moss or sawdust for two or three days, or completely soak the plants in water overnight. Don't let roots dry out when planting. Carry them to the planting site in a wheelbarrow or bucket half-filled with water.

If you can't plant right away because of weather conditions or time schedule, wrap the entire soaked plant in wet burlap or newspaper. Store in a dark, cool spot (between 33° and 60° F.). After a week, if you still can't plant, soak the bushes again for an hour, rewrap, and store again for up to a week.

If you must keep them even longer, soak once again and bury them in a trench at a 45-degree angle, covering the tops completely with a few inches of moist soil. They'll hold like this for up to 5 or 6 weeks. Or store them in a large container of moist peat moss in a shaded, protected area.

Planting bareroot roses

After preparing the hole as outlined earlier, prune the soaked rose plant to three or four strong canes, cutting about ¼ inch above a good bud. (See pruning, page 55.)

Next, prune the main root pieces to reveal white tissue. These cuts will cause scarring, which will promote increased root production.

Build a cone of soil mixture in the center of the hole to support the spread-out roots and hold the plant so the bud union is at the proper ground level. Exact height of the bud

Bareroot rose ready for planting. Plant has been reduced to four healthy canes.

Cut main roots to reveal white tissue. Resulting scarring will give rise to more roots.

After soil is added and tamped, fill hole with water to settle soil around the roots.

Place roots over a cone of soil and use a level pole to determine position of bud union.

Loosely cover plant with soil at least ⅔ of its height to protect from sun and wind.

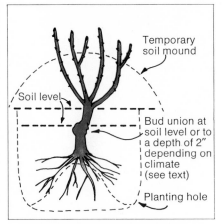

Temporary soil mound

Soil level

Bud union at soil level or to a depth of 2" depending on climate (see text)

Planting hole

union is a point of disagreement among rosarians, even those within the same region. The general rule of thumb is that the budhead should be as much as 2 inches below the soil level in cold winter areas. Place it at or slightly above soil levels in mild winter areas. In mild climates some still advocate placing the budhead below the soil level, while others prefer positioning it up to two inches above the ground. An exposed budhead encourages basal breaks and makes control of suckers and crown gall easier. Whatever method you choose, use a pole or shovel handle to represent soil level when positioning the plant.

With the plant in position, add about ⅔ of the soil mix, then fill the hole with water. Let it soak in completely. Fill in around the roots with soil mix and firm gently.

Mound soil at least ⅔ the height of the plant. You may have to get extra soil for this. Moisten again. This mound gives protection from drying winds and warm sun, and provides enough moisture for the developing plant.

Leave the mound until new growth is one or two inches long, then carefully remove it to the ground level and add mulch.

Planting roses grown in containers

Dig a hole several inches wider and deeper than the container in which the rose is growing. Mix soil in the manner outlined on page 43 and place about six inches in the bottom of the hole.

Remove the plant from the container. If it is a metal can, the nursery will slit the sides for you to make removal easier.

Place the rose in the prepared hole at the same level it was growing in the container. Add the soil mixture around the root soil.

When partially filled, compact the surrounding soil to eliminate air pockets. (See page 42.) Continue to fill in the hole and pack the soil.

Use water to do the final soil compacting and irrigation. Since the rose is already growing, there is no need to mound soil as in the bareroot planting.

Add mulch to prevent rapid drying and soil crusting. Keep well watered until established.

When you move a rose

Transplant roses in the early spring or late fall when they are as dormant as possible, but while the ground is workable.

Prepare the new planting site as you would for planting container-grown roses.

Soak the soil around the rose bush overnight so you can dig the plant with as much earth as possible minimizing root disturbance. Prune large bushes back to 18 to 24 inches to make handling easier.

Position the plant in the new hole and firm soil around the roots.

Irrigate the plant just like you do for bareroot or container-grown plantings.

Label your plants

Roses come with name tags attached. But the wire attachment can damage the cane as it grows. Remove it at planting time, attach the label to a

Prepare a hole several inches wider and deeper than the container in which the rose is growing.

Remove the plant from its container. Leave the soil intact around the plant's roots.

Position the plant in hole and fill in soil. Then tamp down to fill in air pockets.

Fill basin with water and let the water do the final compacting and irrigation.

Top: Pour gravel into bottom of pot.
Bottom: Add some soil, then the plant.

Position plant to its proper growing
height and add more soil mixture.

Irrigate well after planting. Consider
annuals around rose for instant color.

stake and place it in the soil near the bush. Many alternative style labels, plain or decorative, are available.

In addition to name tags near the plant in the garden, make a diagram of your landscape and write in the names of the roses, date planted, source, and any other information. This may be valuable in the years to come, either for yourself or someone else who may live in your home.

Planting and growing full-sized roses in containers

Select a container that gives the root system as much freedom as possible. It must be at least 18 inches in diameter and 24 inches deep. The plant will become rootbound and constricted in a smaller container, resulting in defoliation, halted flower production, or even death.

Wooden tubs and boxes are excellent for roses. Moisture can evaporate through the sides and the soil stays cool. Porous terracotta or glazed pottery also make good containers. Plastic pots are acceptable, but beware of metal containers. The summer heat can cook the roots.

Whatever your choice in containers, be sure to provide good drainage. Several holes in the bottom are ideal. Cleats, casters, feet, wooden x's, or small pieces of brick underneath the

containers help keep the pot from sitting in water. Gravel in the bottom of the pots makes drainage faster.

Plant in a growing medium composed of three parts sandy loam and one part organic matter such as peat moss or leaf mold. Good results are also obtained with any of the soilless mixes, available ready-mixed in large bags. You'll need to be very religious with your fertilizing program if you use the synthetic soils.

Plant either bareroot bushes or plants already growing in cardboard containers or nursery cans. Roses that have a head start seem to adapt best to container gardening. Perhaps it's because their roots have already adjusted to a confined space, while bareroot plants come directly from fields.

When you're ready to plant, place curved pieces of broken crock over the drainage holes to keep soil from washing through. (If you choose a porous clay pot, soak it for about 30 minutes before planting, so the clay won't rob the roots of soil moisture.) Pour in a few inches of fine gravel, crushed volcanic stone, charcoal, or broken pottery for drainage.

Add a few scoops of soil, and set plant at proper growing height (see diagram on page 45). Continue adding soil, packing it in well to eliminate air pockets (page 42). Leave a few inches between the soil level and top of the pot for easier watering. Fill this

reservoir with water and let it soak in to finish compacting the soil.

You can elect to cover the topsoil with a mulch, plant a shallow-rooted ground cover such as Scotch moss or baby's-tears, or add a few annual transplants to dress up the container and provide color before the roses start to bloom.

Care of container plants

Place the container where the bush will get at least six hours of direct morning or midday sunlight. If the bush leans toward the sun, find a lighter place and rotate the pot every few days to keep the plant growing evenly. Keep the plant away from light-colored walls during hot sunny days. Reflected heat can cause foliage burn.

Keep the soil evenly moist at all times during the growing season. Usually twice-a-week watering is sufficient, but the plant may require daily watering during a hot spell. The more active its growth, the more water it will require.

Fertilizing container roses

Feed the plant weekly with liquid plant food. Start with half strength until good growth is established, then increase to full strength as recommended on the label. If you prefer, apply time-release fertilizers every 3-4 months, or use a special combination fertilizer-pesticide product every 6 weeks. (See pages 49-50.)

When the temperature falls below 28° F., place the plant in an unheated shelter away from frost and chilling winds. When the bush begins to defoliate, remove all the foliage and bring the pot indoors. Keep the rose away from windows or heat sources where it might be fooled into thinking it's time to start its growth cycle again. Water occasionally during dormancy, just so soil doesn't dry out. Do not feed. After danger of frost is over, move the pot outdoors. Prune lightly to initiate new growth.

In mild areas where the temperature stays above 28° F. the plant can live outdoors all year. Cut back its water and eliminate feeding during winter months to induce dormancy.

Eliminating weeds, plus...

Soil around roses requires just enough cultivation to eliminate weeds and prevent the tight surface crusts that sometimes form. Cultivating soil to a very shallow level will prevent injury to roots that may be growing close to the surface. Deep cultivation can destroy feeder roots.

Weeds can be controlled by hand pulling or cutting them at soil surface, eliminating cultivation if there's no problem with soil crusting.

Chemical weed control should be practiced according to directions on the manufacturer's weed-control product label. The easy way is to combine chemical weed control, nutrients, and pesticides in one application of systemic rose care (see page 50). Be sure to follow suggested distances from fruit trees and vegetable gardens.

Mulches provide the plus

The role of mulching in rose culture cannot be overemphasized. Look at what mulch does for you:

✓ Eliminates continual cultivation of soil.

✓ Controls weeds.

✓ Retains soil moisture.

✓ Keeps soil temperature more even in both summer and winter.

✓ Cuts down damage from alternative freezing and thawing of winter soil.

✓ Prevents soil crusting and erosion.

✓ Renews and rebuilds humus content of soils (if the mulch is organic).

✓ Encourages root growth.

✓ Activates helpful earthworms and bacteria in the soil.

✓ Completes the landscape design with a neat, manicured look.

Apply mulch after a new planting

A most attractive mulch of bark chips around a freshly planted rose.

Mulching materials

Material	Comments
Bark	Available commercially in chip form or finely ground. Very attractive and long lasting.
Buckwheat hulls	Very attractive, but tend to scatter in windy locations.
Cotton screenings, peanut hulls, shredded tobacco stems	Fairly durable. Supply plant nutrients and improve soil structure. Obtainable from processing plants and mills.
Grass clippings or hay	Probably the most available mulch, but unattractive. Let dry before spreading. Repeated use builds up reserve of available nutrients which lasts for years.
Gravel or stone chips	Not too attractive with roses. Extremely durable, holds down weeds, but does not supply plant nutrients or humus.
Ground corn cobs	Excellent for improving soil structure.
Mushroom compost (spent)	This material is often available in areas where commercial mushrooms are produced. It is usually inexpensive, with a good color that blends into the landscape.
Newspaper	Readily available. Can be used shredded or in sheets, held in place by rocks, bricks, or soil. Cover with more attractive material. Builds humus, and ink contains beneficial trace elements.
Peat moss	Attractive at first, tends to lose esthetic appeal wih age. Available, but expensive for large areas. Compacts and sheds rain water. Should be kept moist at all times.
Pecan hulls	Extremely durable, availability limited.
Pine needles	Will not mat down. Fairly durable. Potential fire hazard.
Black plastic film	Excellent mulch, but unattractive. Can be covered with thin layer of bark. Punch holes for penetration of water. Eliminates weeds entirely.
Rotted manure	May contain weed seeds.
Sawdust, wood chips or shavings	Low in plant nutrients, decompose slowly, tend to pack down. Rose foliage may yellow; additional nitrogen will correct the problem. Well-rotted material preferred. Can be fresh if nitrate of ammonia or nitrate of soda is supplemented at the rate of one pound per 100 square feet. Keep away from building foundations; may attract termites.
Straw	Long-lasting. Depletes nitrogen, but furnishes considerable potassium.
Tree leaves (whole or shredded)	Excellent source of humus. Rot rapidly, high in nutrients.

to a depth of two to four inches. In the past, mulch was put out and taken up before and after every growing season. But tests have proven that it is advantageous to keep the mulch in place all year. As organic mulches decay into the soil, keep them refurbished with additional applications.

If there has been a disease problem, remove all the old mulch and replace it with clean, fresh material in early fall.

There's a wide range of mulching materials to choose from. It's all a matter of availability, cost, ease of handling, and personal preference.

If there's danger of bringing in weed seed with organic mulch materials, either select another mulch or fumigate the material before applying.

Our chart (see page 47) will give you some suggestions for mulches, pointing out their good and bad properties.

Providing fuel for rose productivity

The rose is a high-powered manufacturing plant. To allow it to develop its full power, it must have a continuous supply of water and plenty of the nutrients used in flower production.

Your plant must have a profusion of leaves if it's expected to bear lots of beautiful roses. It takes 25 to 35 perfect leaves to create one perfect rosebud and bring it into bloom. Powered by sunlight, the leaves convert nutrients and water into fuel for growth and flower production.

You can't give a rose too much water

One thing rose people do agree on is that you can't give a rose too much water. But a rose will not tolerate wet feet! Drainage must be excellent. (See page 43.)

Rose foliage will wilt if water is insufficient. Always keep moisture level where the leaves will be distended with water, or "moisture-turgid."

We can't tell you how much or how often to water. The frequency of watering, as well as the amount, depends on soil type, climate, and the growth stage of the rose. More water is needed when the soil is loose and sandy, when it's heavily compacted, when the air is hot and dry, or when new plants are developing.

Normally a rose should receive the equivalent of one inch of rainfall per week, all at one time, starting in early spring and continuing through fall. Hot and dry weather may call for watering every three or four days, or more often during drought. Even when rainfall is plentiful, porous soils benefit from additional deep soakings.

In the early spring, water roses from overhead to prevent canes from drying while developing. When foliage growth begins, keep water off the leaves and apply directly to soil for best results.

When you water, water well, soaking the soil to a depth of 8 to 10 inches. A light sprinkling is worse than no water at all. Frequent light applications result in shallow root systems and increased susceptibility to drought conditions.

Rosarians cannot agree on the correct method of watering. You have a choice—sprinkling or several forms of irrigation.

Some people build a basin or dike around the entire bed, others prefer a basin around each rose bush. Either way the basin is flooded with water that slowly soaks into the soil. This is a good method in dry-summer regions.

The most efficient system seems to be slow-drip irrigation at the base of the plants. A heavy stream of water from a hose is wasteful, because most of it runs off, and what remains pene-

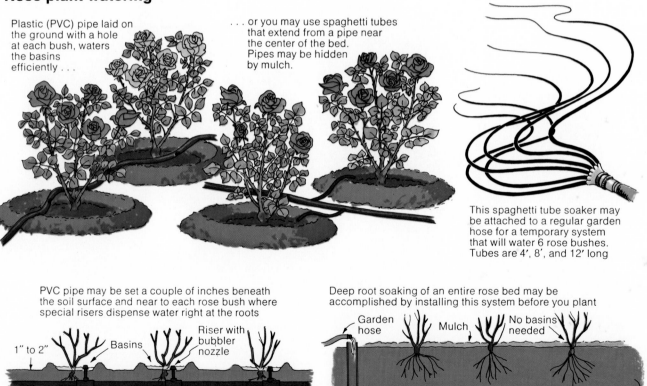

Rose plant watering

Plastic (PVC) pipe laid on the ground with a hole at each bush, waters the basins efficiently . . .

. . . or you may use spaghetti tubes that extend from a pipe near the center of the bed. Pipes may be hidden by mulch.

This spaghetti tube soaker may be attached to a regular garden hose for a temporary system that will water 6 rose bushes. Tubes are 4', 8', and 12' long

PVC pipe may be set a couple of inches beneath the soil surface and near to each rose bush where special risers dispense water right at the roots

1" to 2"   Basins   Riser with bubbler nozzle

Deep root soaking of an entire rose bed may be accomplished by installing this system before you plant

Garden hose   Mulch   No basins needed

Sewer pipe & elbow   Perforated drain pipe   2" of gravel above & below pipe

trates the soil only a few inches. A soaker hose, or one of the methods illustrated below, can provide deep soaking to moisten the soil to the required depth. Also, this system does not wet the foliage or spread the mulch, thus reducing disease. It saves you time, energy, and even money, because less water is used in the long run.

If you do choose to sprinkle, however, water early in the morning so the leaves can dry before they are exposed to the hot midday sun. Be sure the sprinkler runs long enough to meet the 8- to 10-inch-deep soak requirements. With this method you'll have to make more frequent application of fungicides to guard against mildew and blackspot.

Choose rose food from a varied menu

A rose is a heavy user of nutrients. Regular applications of fertilizer are required for optimum growth.

The rate, frequency, and kind of fertilizer depend on the type of soil. Plants in sandy soils benefit from frequent applications, those in heavy soils may not need as much. A soil test can help determine the particular balance of nitrogen, phosphorus, and potassium you need. Or check with your County Extension Agent or nurseryman for recommendations of fertilizer ratio and application rates for your local area.

Begin your fertilizer program for newly planted bushes after the plants become established, about three or four weeks after planting.

Some rose people advocate three applications per year for hybrid teas, grandifloras, and floribundas:

Early spring, just after pruning when bush begins to leaf out.

Early summer, when plant is beginning to flower.

Late summer, to carry them on through fall. In warm coastal areas an additional application in the fall may be necessary.

(A single application per year, early in spring before leaves come out, is usually enough for climbers and shrub species.)

The majority of rosarians agree on more frequent applications for all types of roses. Beginning in early spring as the bush puts out leaves, then continuing every six weeks, or even once each month, through late summer.

There are several types of fertilizers from which to choose, both organic and inorganic. Most people opt for the inorganic because it has controlled reliability, comes formulated specifically for roses, and is easy to obtain.

Liquid food is the exclusive favorite of quite a few rosarians. Many more prefer liquid on newly planted bushes, applied every two to three weeks until the plant is established, then switch to granular fertilizers for a regular diet.

When using liquid rose food, follow the label directions for mixing. Unless the product is recommended for foliar feeding, wash off any liquid fertilizer that remains on the foliage.

Foliar feeding is the method of spraying food directly on foliage, where it is used immediately by the leaves, bypassing the root system of distribution. Some rose growers combine foliar feeding with their regular pesticide spraying every two weeks. The addition of some foliar food just before the peak of the blooming season can result in roses of exhibition quality. Do not apply foliar food in hot weather.

If you select granular fertilizers, be sure to wet the soil before applying. Apply about 6 inches away from the main stem. Distribute the prescribed amount uniformly out beyond branch spread and work into surface of soil or mulch. Water well after application.

Granular fertilizers can be used alone, or in combination with systemic pesticides formulated for use every six weeks during growing season, as described on page 50.

The important thing about fertilizers is to maintain a consistent program. You like your meals on time when you're hungry; so does the rose. And whatever type you choose, pay close attention to the label directions. Overfertilization can cause damage.

Overfertilizing can leave deposits of salts in the soil that cause stunted growth, off-color foliage, and death of new foliage. Water heavily to put salts in suspension, then follow by another heavy watering to leach salts out of the soil.

Ingredients in a balanced plant diet

Elements	Contributions	Signs of Malnutrition
Primary elements		
Nitrogen	Promotes green growth—good canes, stems, leaves. (Too much overstimulates foliage growth at expense of flowers.)	Yellow leaves No new growth Failure of buds to open Small, pale flowers
Phosphorus	Good root growth and flower production	Dull green foliage Falling leaves Weak stems Abnormal root system Slow-to-open buds
Potassium	Vigorous growth	Yellow leaf margins, turning brown Weak stems Underdeveloped buds
Secondary elements		
Calcium	Growth of plant cells and good roots	Deformed growth and abnormal root development
Magnesium	Good growth	Mature yellow leaves, tinged maroon
Sulfur	Green growth	Yellowing of new leaves
Trace elements		
Boron	Good form	Small, curled, and scorched leaves Dead terminal buds
Chlorine	Good growth	Malformed foliage
Copper	Good growth	Poorly developed tips
Iron	Keeps plants green	Yellow foliage
Manganese	Increases nitrogen	Pale mottling of leaves
Molybdenum	Good growth	Poorly developed leaves
Zinc	Good growth	Malformed growth

Note: Malnutrition, deficiency, or overabundance do not occur in plants that are given properly balanced fertilizers for the particular soil.

Coping with pests and diseases

Take a leisurely walk through your garden every few days and enjoy the beautiful rewards of your labor. At the same time keep an eye out for early signs of trouble, such as wilted foliage, deformed flower buds, or spots on leaves.

If you discover any such warnings, don't jump to the conclusion that your garden is disease or pest-ridden—unless of course you find some insects. Take time to diagnose the problem. Remember that many plant troubles can be caused by poor gardening practices. Not enough water can cause wilt, too much water can cause rot, alkaline soil can cause yellow leaves. Make sure the problem is not a cultural one before spraying unnecessarily.

Prevention is the key word

Remember, a rose that is growing vigorously can withstand more injury from unwanted invaders than a rose that is under stress from lack of water or nutrients.

Some diseases can be prevented by correct watering practices, as outlined on page 48. Avoid watering the entire rose bush, which can cause mildew. Water only the soil underneath the bush. When using the hose, avoid splattering soil or mulch. This spreads powdery mildew or blackspot.

Losses from diseases can be minimized by obtaining the best quality rose plants, those that show no abnormal swellings on the roots or crowns and are free of discolored areas on stems. Buy from reliable sources who guarantee their product to be disease-free. Choose cultivars with built-in disease-resistance. There are many from which to choose.

Practice maintenance pruning. Remove all canes showing cankers as soon as you detect them. Be sure to destroy the prunings. Remove and destroy individual leaves bearing black spots as soon as you detect them.

Don't forget a winter cleanup. You will find that there'll be fewer insects and disease organisms to combat when the new leaves unfurl in the spring if you do a thorough cleanup job when roses are dormant. To keep rust and blackspot from carrying over from year to year, strip all leaves from your bushes. Rake up any leaves that have fallen, and burn or dump them in the garbage can. Spray the canes and the soil or mulch beneath with a specially formulated dormant spray. Drench twigs and canes.

Set up a regular spray schedule for disease and pest control during the growing season. You may never even see any pests or disease evidence if you follow a regular program of preventive spraying or dusting of the plants with a multipurpose pesticide every couple of weeks during the growing season. On the average this takes about an hour per week to care for most rose gardens.

An alternative approach to spraying is to use systemics. You can give the plant the power to protect itself from its worst enemies when you apply a systemic to the soil. You save even more time and energy when you use products that combine nutrients with pesticides.

There will be no need for routine spraying for the normal attacks of aphids, spider mites, white flies, leaf-mining insects, leafhoppers and other sucking types, if a systemic is applied

Follow a routine spraying program during growing season or spray to combat invasions.

every six weeks. The plant then has internal protection that cannot be washed off by rain or water from sprinklers. And beneficial insects such as lady bugs and bees go unharmed.

However, there may be times when you are faced with an invasion of pests and need additional help. In such cases it's important to act quickly. Spray or dust at the very first sign of attack. Get the first aphids, the first brood of beetles, the first invasion of thrips, and you'll minimize the use of sprays.

Using chemical controls

When you do use sprays, let your common sense guide you. The following pointers are intended to help you learn how to use the best that modern research has to offer in the war against garden problems.

1. Observe all directions and precautions on pesticide labels. They are

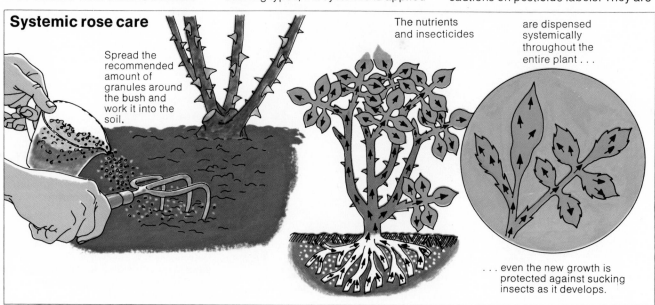

Systemic rose care

Spread the recommended amount of granules around the bush and work it into the soil.

The nutrients and insecticides

are dispensed systemically throughout the entire plant . . .

. . . even the new growth is protected against sucking insects as it develops.

Blackspot

Crown gall

Aphid

Japanese beetle

Mildew

there for your benefit.

2. Store all chemical products behind locked doors, in their original containers with labels intact. Keep them away from foodstuffs and out of the reach of children and pets.

3. Use pesticides at correct dosage and intervals to avoid unnecessary residues and injury to plants and animals. Never use a stronger spray than is recommended by the manufacturer. The sprays have been carefully formulated by experts to do the most effective job.

4. Mix chemicals in an open area. Spray on calm days to prevent drifts. Work on the windward side when applying. Be fully clothed when spraying, and avoid prolonged inhalation of any chemical.

5. Dispose of surplus pesticides and used containers so that contamination of water and other hazards will not result. Wrap in paper and place in garbage cans.

6. After handling pesticides, be sure to wash up before you eat, drink, or smoke.

Some states have restrictions on the use of certain chemical controls. Check your state and local regulations if you have any doubt.

Use your county agent

Don't hesitate to ask your local County Extension Service for help and recommendations in combating pests and diseases. Your local agent keeps abreast of current studies going on at your state university research stations and has the answers to questions on problems peculiar to your area.

Let nature help

In addition to help from pesticides, you might want to call on a couple of nature's helpers to aid in outsmarting the spoilers. Introduce some beneficial insects into the garden. Predacious insects such as lady bug beetles, praying mantis, Tricho-

gramma wasps, and lacewings can help keep the population of aphids and other pests under control. Either leave a couple of bushes unsprayed as a haven for these good guys, or rely on systemic pesticides applied to the soil and taken up in the sap stream which do not harm them.

Birds can be a menace to the vegetable garden or fruit orchard, but they can be a delightful asset to the rose garden. Insect-eating species include bluebirds, chickadees, mockingbirds, orioles, robins, wrens, and warblers. Encourage their visits with bird feeders hung near the roses.

The charts on the next two pages describe specific rose trouble symptoms, identify the problem, and make some suggested solutions.

Other pests

Ants are often seen following the paths of aphids to eat the sticky honey residue. They may build nests in the ground which can disturb the rose roots. Use Diazinon to eradicate.

Outsmarting the spoilers

Symptoms		Problems	Solutions
Clusters of tiny insects on young shoots, flower buds, or underside of leaves. Foliage and blooms stunted or deformed. Sticky honeydew left behind attracts ants.	Enlarged 2x	APHIDS. Soft-bodied, green, brown, or reddish insects that suck plant juices.	Harmless lady beetles added to the garden will feed on aphids. Wipe out infestations with contact sprays such as Diazinon, Malathion, Sevin, ORTHENE.
Foliage, flowers, and stems are chewed, devoured, or have holes drilled in them.	All life size	BEETLES (including, 1. Japanese, 2. rose chafer, 3. rose curculio, and 4. Fuller beetles). Their larvae also eat plant roots.	Pick off beetles by hand or knock them into a can of kerosene and water. Spray with Sevin, Diazinon, or Malathion.
Circular black spots with fringed margins appear on leaves. Leaves may turn yellow and drop prematurely. On more resistant varieties, leaves will remain green and hang onto bush.		BLACKSPOT. A fungus disease, easily spread to nearby bushes by rain or hose. Overwinters in small cane lesions or leaves left on ground.	Water with wand or soil soaker. If you must wet foliage, do it from overhead and early in day, so bush can dry before night. Apply fungicides such as PHALTAN and Captan.
Grayish-brown growth on buds and partially opened flowers, especially pink and white hybrid teas. The diseased flowers come apart easily when touched.		BOTRYTIS BLIGHT. A fungus disease that overwinters on infected plant parts.	Pick off and destroy faded and infected blooms. Spray with fungicides. Read labels for recommendations.
Flower buds eaten or leaves rolled and tied around the pest, eaten from inside. Most often a late spring problem.	Life size	BUDWORM AND OTHER CATERPILLARS. Larvae of moths and butterflies that feed on rose foliage.	Cut out infested buds and leaves. Apply Diazinon, Sevin, or ORTHENE.
Holes eaten into leaves from the underside, causing a skeletonized glazed effect. Appear early in the spring. Later, large holes eaten in leaves and, finally, the veins are devoured.	Approx. life size	BRISTLY ROSE SLUGS (Often called cane borers or leafworms.) Half-inch long, hairy, slimy larvae of sawfly; when young, eat underside of leaves, when mature, eat entire leaf.	Act quickly to stop their speedy damage. Spray with Sevin.
Lesions in the woody tissue of a cane, poor growth, or death above the affected area.		CANKER. A disease caused by parasitic fungus that usually enters plant through wounds or dying tissue.	Prune out and burn all affected areas, cutting well below canker with shears dipped in alcohol after each cut. Paint with pruning paint or spray. Same treatment as for blackspot will help.
Roundish, rough-surfaced growths near plant's crown or on roots. Plants lose vigor, produce abnormal flowers and foliage, and eventually die.		CROWN GALL. Soil-borne bacterial disease which can live on in soil after affected plant is removed and may or may not affect a new plant.	Do not buy plants with swellings near bud union or on roots. Remove and burn infected parts, seal with pruning paint. Or remove entire bush and treat soil with all-purpose fumigant before setting new plants.
Top surface of leaves turns pale and becomes covered with tiny yellow specks similar to damage of spider mites.	Life size / Enlarged 3x	LEAFHOPPERS. Tiny, greenish yellow, jumping insects found on underside of leaves. They suck out contents of leaf cells.	Apply Diazinon or Malathion.
Pale green foliage and stunted growth in spite of good gardening practices. Root examination reveals abnormal swelling, knotty enlargements with tiny white eggs inside, discolored lesions, or dead tissue.	Enlarged approx. 5x / Eggs	NEMATODES. Disease caused by tiny animal pests that invade the roots of the plant.	Check with your County Agent or Agricultural Experiment Station for help in diagnosis and control. All-purpose soil fumigants or nematocides are beneficial.

Symptoms		Problems	Solutions
Holes in cut ends of canes or punctures in stems. Wilting of plant shoot, foliage, and canes. Sometimes slight swelling of canes.	1. 2. 3.	PITHBORERS (including, 1. rose stem sawfly, 2. rose stem girdler, and 3. small carpenter bees). Pests bore into cane and lay eggs. Larvae eat through canes.	Cut out canes below infested portion during spring pruning. Seal exposed tips with pruning paint.
White powdery masses of spores on young leaves, shoots, and buds; distorted young shoots; stunted foliage.		POWDERY MILDEW. Disease spread by wind. Encouraged by warm days followed by cool nights. Overwinters on fallen leaves and inside stems and bud scales.	Apply Parnon or PHALTAN. For best results, apply when mildew is first noticed.
Large mossy or callus swellings on stems, or roots. Look like crown gall, but if cut open, you'll find larvae. (Mostly on species roses.)		ROSE GALL (including mossy rose gall, and rose root gall). Caused by wasplike insects that bore into canes and lay eggs. The growing larvae cause swelling.	Insecticides do not control. Prune infested stems and burn to destroy larvae before they emerge. Seal exposed area.
Black, deformed flower buds and leaves that die prematurely.	Enlarged 3x	ROSE MIDGE. Tiny, yellowish flies lay eggs in growing tips of stems. Hatching maggots destroy tender tissue.	Remove and destroy affected areas. Spray with ORTHENE.
Wilting and darkening of foliage, which drops prematurely. Close examination reveals mature stems encrusted with hard-shelled insects.	Approx. life size	ROSE SCALES. Round, dirty white, gray, or brown shell-covered insects that suck sap from plants.	Prune out and destroy old, infested wood. Apply Malathion, Sevin, ORTHENE, Dormant Oil Spray.
Wilted leaves that may drop. Yellow dots and light green mottling appear on upper leaf surface opposite pustules of powdery, rust-colored spores on the lower surface.		RUST. Overwinters in fallen leaves, spread by wind. The disease is especially troublesome along the Pacific Coast.	Remove and destroy all rusted leaves during pruning. Apply lime-sulfur spray as a dormant spray. Select rust-resistant varieties when planting new roses.
Stippled leaves appear dry, turn brown, red, yellow, or gray, then curl and drop off. Sometimes webs are visible on the underside of leaves.		SPIDER MITES. Minute pests that suck juices from underside of rose foliage. Abundant in hot, dry weather.	Clean up trash and weeds in early spring to destroy breeding places. Spray infestations with Diazinon, ORTHENE, Malathion, Dormant Oil Spray.
White spots with dark red rims, turning yellow. Leaves develop holes and fall off. There may be brown raised spots on stems.		SPOT ANTHRACNOSE. A fungus disease. Overwinters in infected stem, and spores are spread by spring rains.	Prune out infected canes in spring. Apply fungicide. Read labels for recommendations.
Flecked petals and deformed flowers, especially on white varieties.		THRIPS. Very active, tiny, slender, brownish-yellow, winged insects. Hide in base of infected flowers.	Cut off and dispose of spent blooms. Apply Diazinon, Malathion, ORTHENE.
Small, angular, colorless spots on foliage. Ring, oakleaf, watermark, or mosaic patterns develop on leaves.		VIRUS DISEASES (including Mosaic). Spread by propagation of infected plants.	Prevention is only control. Do not buy any plants exhibiting the symptoms described. Dispose of entire affected plants to prevent spread of virus to other nearby plants.

Deer love to feed on tender young rose shoots. Garden centers have repellents that are available to spray on foliage or apply to the soil around the planting area.

Leafcutter bees make perfect circles and ovals in rose leaves during the summer. There's no control for the leaf damage. Since the bee doesn't eat the cut-out portion, but uses it to line nests, poisons are not effective. Even if they were, we wouldn't want to harm these bees that are integral in natural pollination. Cut out any wilted or dying shoots that may have been used as nests.

Moles can disturb roots with their tunneling when searching for food, causing unhealthy growth or even death in rose plants. Mole traps are available, or you can treat the soil with a soil insecticide like Diazinon to kill many of the soil insects on which moles feed.

Pine mice burrow underground and cut off roots. Watch for small exit holes and speedy run-off of water. Place poisoned food inside the holes, and cover with pieces of tile or boards to protect other animals.

Conquering chlorosis

Chlorosis is an unnatural yellowing of rose foliage, with the veins usually staying darker green. It is caused by an iron shortage resulting from poor drainage, excess lime in the soil, naturally alkaline soils, or lack of organic matter. Proper preparation of the planting site based on results of a soil test is the best prevention. (See page 43.)

Roses with some yellow or orange shadings in the petals are most susceptible to chlorosis. Spraying the leaves with liquid iron will take care of mild cases.

For severe cases try one of the following remedies:

1. Improve soil conditions by mixing manure and agricultural sulfur into the surface soil. Use ratio of two pounds sulfur to a cubic foot of manure.

2. Bore a tiny hole into all canes that are ½ inch or larger in diameter and fill with iron citrate. Seal the hole with pruning paint.

3. Add soluble iron to the roots. Make 3- to 6-inch-deep holes in moist soil in the root area. Put about 1 ounce of ferrous (iron) sulfate in each hole and cover with soil. Apply ½ to 1 pound per bush, depending upon plant size. Each irrigation will diffuse enough soluble iron to the root system to supply the plant. One treatment is usually effective for up to four years.

4. Apply one of the more expensive chelated irons. Follow manufacturer's directions.

Protection from the elements

Any strong wind is bad for roses. Even brisk ocean breezes can damage nearby plants. And the salt spray in the air isn't welcomed. A hedge of protective shrubs or a fence helps shield the roses.

If a wind is hot and dry, there's a lot of trouble in store for roses. A screen of shrubs or trees that slows the wind down and contributes some moisture to the wind as it passes through is a big help in such cases.

A fence won't do the job. Air on the leeward side of a fence is more turbulent than on the leeward side of a hedge. And most important, a fence doesn't add moisture to dry air like a shrub does.

Allow at least ten feet between rose bushes and a screen or hedge. Select deep-rooted shrubs that fare well in your climate. Ask your nurseryman how close to space them together so they will form a solid screen.

Hot weather fatigues a rose plant. At temperatures above 90° F., the plant uses food faster than its leaf factory can manufacture it. If you live in a hot climate, don't prune back roses as much as rosarians do in cooler environments. During the winter prune only enough to shape the plants the way you want them. The plant needs to be big when spring comes so photosynthesis has a chance to build the plant up before summer heat comes.

In extremely hot sunny areas, you might consider adding a lath covering over at least a portion of the rose garden to give some shade during the hottest part of the day.

Cool nights or dark, damp days can cause "balling" or half-opened blooms. Cut off such blooms when they start to ball in order to allow for better new growth when weather conditions improve.

If you live in a cool or foggy area, select rose varieties with fewer petals to insure opening.

Sudden changes in temperature in the fall, before the plant has hardened off for winter, can be disastrous. Early freezes kill more canes than much colder winter freezes. In areas with chances of early freezes, avoid late summer feedings and hold back on water.

Freezes in late winter or early spring kill shoots that have been forced during warm winter days. Don't prune until all danger of frost is past.

Sometimes, after very mild or warm winters, branch tips may remain bare or the side buds on some canes fail to open. They were not chilled enough to induce normal growth. Prune out such canes.

In extremely warm regions, prune in winter and remove by hand all leaves from the plants, forcing a period of dormancy.

Protect container roses from flooding during heavy rains by moving to a sheltered area or securing heavy duty plastic covering around the stems and over the top of the pot.

When you grow roses for exhibition, injury from winds or rains can ruin everything. Hot sunshine can fade the colors just before show time.

To protect specimen blooms, cover them with light plastic bags clipped together at the bottom. Be sure to leave enough opening for air passage.

Or, make a cone-shaped cap of plastic or heavy paper and attach it to stakes next to the plant to cover bloom. Move the cap as needed with clips hooked to the stake. To delay a bud opening or to hold a color longer, use caps of black paper or dark plastic.

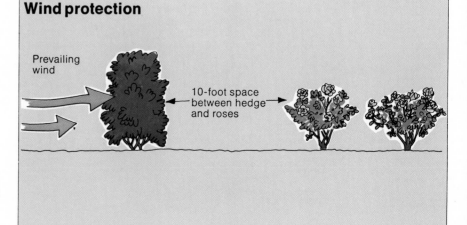

Wind protection

Prevailing wind

10-foot space between hedge and roses

All replacement growth comes from buds or "eyes" that are found on sides of canes at the base of leaf or just above the leaf scar. Look for single buds (left) and make pruning cuts ¼ inch above. Eliminate any double buds (right) during pruning to prevent undesirable double-headed cane growth.

Pruning bush roses for better production

An unpruned rose can grow into a mass of tangled brambles that produces small or inferior blooms. Proper pruning removes nonproductive or damaged wood, and leaves a few good canes as the foundation of a healthy bush. Pruning gives the rose plant an attractive shape and desired size that fits into the landscape design. And the flower quality is improved by good pruning practices.

When to prune?

Prune just before the rose bush breaks dormancy. The right time can fall anytime between January in warm areas to April in very cold zones. Check with your County Extension Service for suggested local dates.

Don't prune roses until you completely remove winter protection and frost danger is past. (Frost can make a second pruning necessary.) Prune before new leaves develop to prevent loss of nutritive sap from cut surfaces.

Use the right equipment

You'll need three types of cutting instruments. Make sure they have sharp blades and are well lubricated.

1. A fine-toothed, curved saw for cutting woody tissue.
2. Pruning shears with one side for cutting and one for holding.

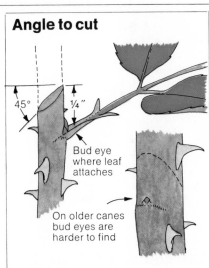

Angle to cut

45°   ¼"

Bud eye where leaf attaches

On older canes bud eyes are harder to find

Use pruning saw to prune woody growth.

Prune small canes and twigs with shears.

Cut heavy canes with long-handled loppers.

3. Long-handled lopping shears for thick canes or getting into hard-to-reach places.

In addition, you'll need a pair of heavy-duty leather garden gloves and pruning paint to seal major cuts.

Make cuts correctly

Cut at sharp 45°-65° angles. Do not leave any bare stubs that can be susceptible to diseases. Make all cuts down to a cane, or to the point on the crown from which the cane originated, or to a strong outside bud or "eye" on stem nodes. This eye is the origin of all new replacement growth. Make cuts about ¼ inch above the bud.

When using pruning shears, make sure the cutting blade is on the lower side to insure a clean cut. The slight injury that results from pressure on the noncutting side should be on the top part of the cane that will be discarded.

How much to prune?

There are three basic types of pruning:

Severe or heavy. The plant is cut back to three or four canes, 6 to 10 inches high. This method is practiced to produce showy blooms. Prune only vigorous, well-established bushes in this manner. Severe pruning of weak bushes sacrifices the plant's vigor and reduces the life span of the bush.

Moderate. 5 to 12 canes are left, about 18 to 24 inches high. Moderate pruning develops a much larger bush than severe pruning and is best suited to most garden roses.

Light. A minimum of cutting, with plants remaining 3 to 4 feet in height. Light pruning produces a profusion of short-stemmed flowers on larger bushes. This method is practiced mainly with floribundas, grandifloras,

Moderate pruning produces larger plants, the best method for landscape roses.

first-year hybrid teas, species roses, or weak-growing varieties of all classes.

Our research found rosarians practicing all three methods within the same climatic zone. It's a matter of preference through experience. It usually takes several years to learn the best method for each variety of rose you prune. Don't be shy when it comes to taking off growth. Most roses are hardy shrubs and will bounce

back with plenty of new growth.

Pruning procedure

You will find heavy pruning easier if the bud union is above ground. If you have planted below the soil level, you might wish to remove soil from around the bud union during pruning so you can see the origin of all canes.

First, remove any dead wood down to the nearest healthy, dormant bud. Make the cut at least one inch below

Unpruned hybrid tea rose.

Cut out old or dead canes and branches.

Remove canes with signs of disease.

This rose bush has been pruned back severely to produce exhibition-quality roses.

Suckers grow from the rootstock below the bud union. They must be completely removed or they will soon dominate the plant. Dig down below the bud union to find the source of the sucker growth. Remove it down to its base, along with part of the crown, if necessary.

the dead area. If no live buds remain, remove the entire branch or cane to the bud union.

Examine carefully for canker or other diseased areas (see pages 50-53). Cut down to a good bud at least an inch below any evidence of disease. Although canes may look healthy, there can be a problem in the pith. Cut the top of each cane and check inside. Pith should be creamy white, not brown or gray. Prune down to where pith is healthy, or to bud union if pith is diseased all the way through.

Cut out weak, spindly, or deformed growth. This includes canes that grow straight out, then curve upward (doglegs). Remove canes growing toward the center of the bush. If two branches cross, remove the weaker one.

Remove all suckers or reversion growth (undesired shoots that come from rootstock below the bud union). Sucker foliage is different in color and form than the rest of the plant. If you do not remove suckers they will soon dominate the plant. When cutting them out, take all of the sucker base from the crown area, along with a piece of the crown if necessary.

Next, thin out remaining healthy canes to desired shape and cut them down to selected height. After severe winters all the canes may have to be cut to within several inches of the bud union. In such cases you can't worry about shape, just save as much live wood as you can.

Seal all major cuts with pruning paint to aid in healing wounds and to keep out insects and diseases.

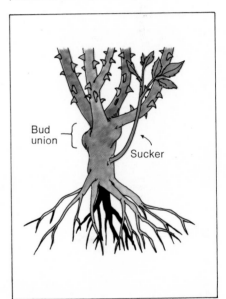

Bud union

Sucker

Remove canes to create desired shape.

Cut back tops to selected height.

Apply pruning paint to all major cuts.

Vigorous Winifred Coulter climber.

Laterals of properly pruned climber are tied in a horizontal position.

Pruning and training climbing roses

Prune ramblers and vigorous climbing roses soon after flowering. Cut out diseased or dead canes and remove older gray canes, as well as weak new ones. Most climber canes are good for only two or three seasons. Save the green healthy canes. Cut laterals back to 8 or 10 buds to shape the plant as desired. Be sure to remove any suckers.

Some of the less vigorous climbers need to be trimmed each spring only to remove winterkill. Later, remove the faded flowers after blooming has stopped.

Hybrid climbers and everblooming large-flowered climbers are pruned while dormant. Do not take as much wood from the everbloomers as the hybrids. Proceed as you would with bush roses: remove dead and diseased canes, get rid of any sucker growth; remove old growth or weak new growth. Retain three or four vigorous young canes.

Keep flowers plucked off ever-blooming roses, but do not take foliage, since reblooming occurs from the top leaves, immediately under the old flower cluster. When removing hybrid blooms, leave two leaf buds on each flowering shoot.

All climbers are pruned to make

Remove all inferior growth.

Strip foliage to reveal growth pattern.

Remove old canes with loppers.

Tie remaining canes to the support.

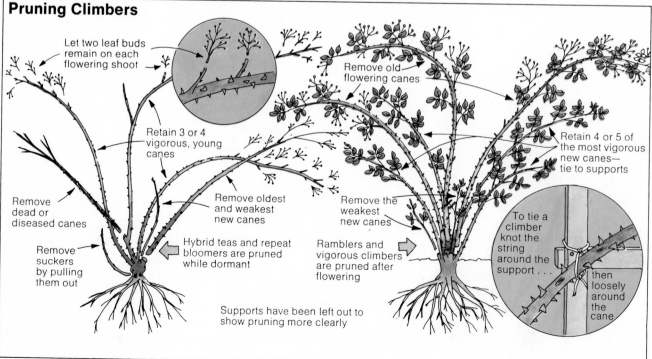

Pruning Climbers

Let two leaf buds remain on each flowering shoot

Retain 3 or 4 vigorous, young canes

Remove dead or diseased canes

Remove suckers by pulling them out

Hybrid teas and repeat bloomers are pruned while dormant

Remove oldest and weakest new canes

Remove old flowering canes

Remove the weakest new canes

Ramblers and vigorous climbers are pruned after flowering

Retain 4 or 5 of the most vigorous new canes— tie to supports

To tie a climber knot the string around the support . . .

then loosely around the cane

Supports have been left out to show pruning more clearly

them fit the place where they are being trained—arbors, fences, pergolas, pillars, trellises. They should be trained by arching or tying them to a horizontal position with tips pointed downward in order to make every bud produce a flowering branch. See diagram for directions on how to tie them up.

Shortening some of the long canes will stimulate laterals to develop and continue to elongate and cover the support.

Pruning tree roses

Standards are pruned just like bush roses. Cut out dead or diseased branches or canes, leaving healthy canes pruned back to a good bud. Keep the shape as symmetrical as possible so the foliage will fill out into a full, round shape.

You have twice as much chance for suckers with tree roses as you do with bush plants. They can grow from the root stock or from the trunk stock. Cut them out as closely to their base as possible.

Pruning old-fashioned, shrub, or species roses

There are many roses that fit into this category and almost as many ways to prune and train. Your best bet is to consult the nursery from which you secure the plant, or read a few of the

books devoted to growing these roses.

Basically there are two methods of pruning:

Annual bloomers should not be pruned until after they have bloomed. Then shorten the long canes by ⅓ and trim up lateral canes only a few inches.

Repeat bloomers should be trimmed to a good shape, not cut back. Keep faded flowers plucked during blooming to encourage growth of new flowering stems.

Don't put away the pruning shears

Prune and groom roses as they grow. Continue all season to cut out weak and spindly shoots, suckers, and obvious signs of disease. Remove old flowers as soon as they have passed their peak.

Flowers of hybrid teas are produced in waves. Allowing the plant to set seeds increases the interval between periods of bloom. In removing fading flowers don't just snip off the flower, but cut back to a 5-leaflet leaf. Cuts at these major leaves result in stronger foliage breaks as the plant continues to develop. During the first growing season of a newly planted rose just snip the flowers; a young plant needs all the leaves it can produce. In cold, winter areas, allow the seed pods (hips) to form on the final wave of bloom. Formation of hips slows

Lightly pruned old garden rose.

down growth and hardens the plant for winter.

Rosarians who want to produce large exhibition blooms disbud most of the side vegetative buds and flowers and allow only one or a selected few terminal buds to mature.

Pruning tree rose

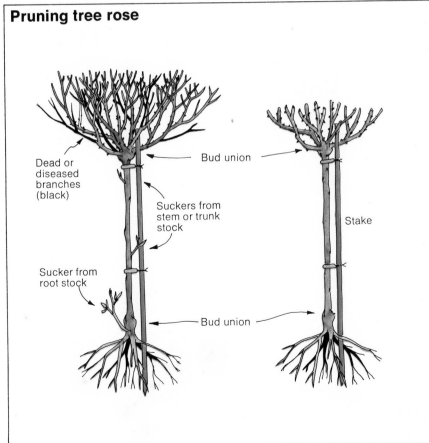

Dead or diseased branches (black)

Bud union

Suckers from stem or trunk stock

Sucker from root stock

Bud union

Stake

Disbudding

Pinch off secondary buds

Cutting

Allow at least two five-leaflet leaves to remain on the new shoot when you cut a rose

Cut here

Prior cuts

Provide winter protection

This is probably the most controversial area of rose culture. Some experts go so far as to advise against any winter protection, except mulch, even in pretty cold climates. On the other side, some people in the same area recommend tipping and burying the entire plant. Once again, we suggest calling upon your County Extension Agent for help in determining what kind of protection may be best for your locality.

Many roses, including quite a few species, shrubs, and climbers, are naturally cold hardy and need little or no protection. There are a number of newer hybrid teas marketed as sub-zero plants that are reported to need little protection. We talked to rosarians who say, however, that they need just as much covering as other hybrids.

One of a plant's best defenses against cold weather is proper summer care. Vigorous bushes are able to withstand cold far better than unhealthy ones. Roses planted in locations that are protected by trees,

A burlap wrapping around straw insulation provides good cold-weather protection. Note soil mounded around base.

In spite of severe winters, recognized rose authority, Dr. Cynthia Wescott, uses only minimum oak leaf natural winter mulch throughout her extensive rose garden.

Cold frame

Hinged top for ventilation on warm days

Banked soil for insulation

Partial covering

Tie canes together and mound soil 12" or more over bud union. Leave exposed until soil freezes . . .

. . . then cover with evergreen boughs or straw to keep mound frozen

A cylinder of wire mesh will hold the soil and insulation in place during wind or rain

Complete covering

Dig up roots on one side . . .

Bend bush over into trench and cover with soil

Do not disturb roots on other side

Burlap wrapping

Evergreen boughs or corn stalks

Bottomless bushel basket

Soil, peat moss, or bark

Burlap cover

Bark or peat moss

Styrofoam rose cone

Rock or brick

Tar-paper cylinder

Soil mound

Wire hook

Soil mound

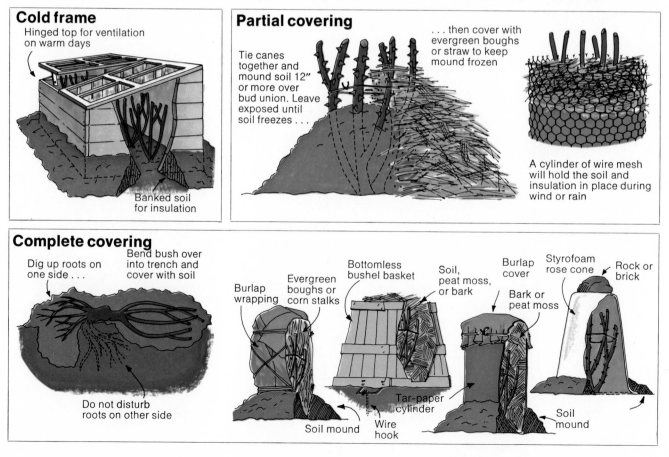

Container soil around climbing roses is covered with pine-bough mulch, reported to be adequate protection.

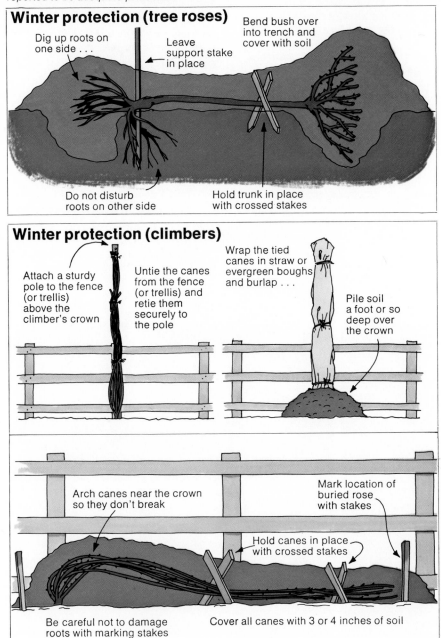

Winter protection (tree roses)

Dig up roots on one side . . .

Leave support stake in place

Bend bush over into trench and cover with soil

Do not disturb roots on other side

Hold trunk in place with crossed stakes

Winter protection (climbers)

Attach a sturdy pole to the fence (or trellis) above the climber's crown

Untie the canes from the fence (or trellis) and retie them securely to the pole

Wrap the tied canes in straw or evergreen boughs and burlap . . .

Pile soil a foot or so deep over the crown

Arch canes near the crown so they don't break

Mark location of buried rose with stakes

Hold canes in place with crossed stakes

Be careful not to damage roots with marking stakes

Cover all canes with 3 or 4 inches of soil

large shrubs, or structures need less protection than bushes exposed to the elements.

Where temperatures drop to 10° to 15° F. for as much as two weeks at a time, most bush roses are adequately protected by mounding the base of each plant with fresh, loose soil or compost that drains well. Immediately after the first frost, mound up soil to a depth of 6 to 8 inches. Some growers advise cutting back plants as much as 16 to 30 inches before mounding. If you do this, be sure to clean up and dispose of all clippings to cut down disease spread. In any case, apply a final coat of dormant spray before mounding. At this time you can tie canes together to protect from winds if you like.

Add hay or straw over the mound and exposed canes after the first hard freeze to protect against fluctuating temperatures, and freezing and thawing of soil around the canes.

There are rose caps available from horticultural houses, or you can devise your own cover. If you elect to use caps, prune the plant to fit underneath.

If you live in an area where salt is used on roads, protect your plants by spreading plastic over the soil after the first hard freeze, then cover with straw or hay.

Where temperatures dip below zero, additional protection may be required. We've illustrated ideas from quite a few rosarians.

Exercise care when you remove winter coverings in the spring. Don't get too anxious. The tender growth underneath is easily killed by even a light freeze. Keep some straw or mulch material handy to cover plants in the event of a late frost.

Tree roses

In mild-winter areas, wrap the plants in straw and cover with burlap. No protection is necessary in temperate zones.

If temperature goes as low as 10° F., dig under the roots in late fall on one side, until the plant can be pulled over on the ground without breaking root connections with the soil. Stake the plant to the ground and cover the entire plant with several inches of soil.

In spring, after soil thaws and frost danger is past, remove soil and set plant upright once again.

Climbing roses

A burlap wrapping is adequate protection in mild-winter climates. But in areas with hard freezes, you can bury climbers the same way you would tree roses.

Miniature roses indoors/outdoors

You can easily grow the miniatures of the rose world someplace around the house all year long. Plant them outdoors either in the ground or in containers, even hanging baskets. Indoors, grow them in a sunny window or under artificial lighting.

Potted miniatures adapt well to mobile gardening. Grow them in a favorable outdoor environment in warm seasons, then bring them indoors and enjoy the blooms. When the flowers fade, return them to the garden to rebloom. Or, put the plants outdoors when weather permits, and bring them inside for a winter garden. Try growing under lights all year and when the plants bloom place them anywhere you want to enjoy the flowers for a few days.

Outdoor culture

The small varieties differ only slightly from large roses in care. Since they grow on their own roots, you don't have to worry about bud unions when you plant. Whether you plant in a pot or in the ground, set the rose bush slightly deeper than it originally grew.

Most varieties should be spaced about 10 to 12 inches apart. Make sure the roses are separated from large plants that can rob them of much-needed sunshine and moisture.

When you read catalog descriptions of miniature plant sizes, remember that these are based on indoor or greenhouse pot culture, where size is

A spray of tiny blooms of Stacey Sue grown under fluorescent lights.

regulated by the restricted root growth. Although the flowers remain tiny, many of the miniature plants will grow quite large when planted in the ground, especially in temperate climates. If you want to keep the bushes small, you'll need to prune back severely.

Pruning is easy. In the spring just clip the plant back, like boxwood, into the desired shape and shake out the clippings. You can prune miniatures back to ½ their size.

These little plants are more cold-resistant than most hybrid teas or other garden roses, and require little winter protection. In warm climates they even keep on blooming all year.

Miniatures can be bedded together or share containers with a host of

small companions. Here are only a few suggestions:

Annuals—alyssum, calendula, lobelia, marigold, fairy primrose, and viola;

Bulbs—crocus, grape-hyacinth, miniature tulips and iris, and narcissus;

Groundcovers—small-leaved ivy, baby's-tears, and sedum;

Herbs—basil, oregano, and parsley;

Vegetables—garlic, kale, leaf lettuce, and Swiss chard;

Other small plants—boxwood and ferns.

Year-round indoor roses

The miniatures will bloom indoors all year, except for about two months' rest. You can expect a cycle of blooms every six to eight weeks. With roses

Outdoor culture for miniatures is almost the same as for the larger roses. Here the miniatures are in a raised bed to make all the chores easier.

If you choose not to grow potted roses indoors during winter, just place the pots in perlite in late fall and leave outdoors. The snow provides good winter protection.

Grow miniatures on a moist pebble tray in a sunny window.

potted up at various times, it's possible to have continual flowering. Select compact, low-growing varieties for indoor use.

Plant in a 4- to 8-inch pot with a mixture of equal parts sterilized garden soil, peat moss (or other organic humus), and coarse sand (or perlite). Be sure the container has excellent drainage. Immerse the freshly planted rose in water just over the pot rim until all bubbling stops.

After planting and soaking, put the bush on a cool porch, in a coldframe, or a cool, protected outdoor area where it can acclimate itself for two to four weeks. When renewed growth begins, bring the plant indoors and place it in a sunny window.

Keep the soil evenly moist, never soggy wet. Occasionally let the surface dry, then water well from the top of the pot. Yellow leaves indicate improper drainage or too much water.

Yellow leaves can also indicate that the surrounding air is too dry. Miniature roses like more moisture than the average house provides. Build up the humidity by keeping the

plant on a tray filled with pebbles or sand. Maintain some water in the bottom of the tray, but not deep enough to reach the bottom of the pot. Routine washing of the foliage in the sink will help add moisture and also remove any residues from sprays or household grease and keep the insect population under control.

Feed with a house plant fertilizer monthly. And follow a preventive spray program, as for regular outdoor roses, to control diseases and pests. (See pages 50-53). The worst enemy of miniature roses is spider mite. Keep an eye out and provide early treatment.

Some growers suggest an annual 8-weeks' rest during the hottest summer months. Place the plant in the hydrator of a refrigerator. After the forced dormancy, cut the plant back to one-half its size and resume normal care.

Prune the plant anytime it's necessary to keep it to the desired shape and size. Cut back to about one-third its height with sharp, clean shears, just above a 5-leaflet leaf. Pinch or trim new shoots to induce branching.

Keep spent blooms pinched off. You may need to repot each year when you repot other plants grown indoors.

Roses under man-made sun

Miniature roses are good candidates for light gardening. The plants remain compact since they never have to reach for the light source, and they're covered with blooms in 6- to 8-week cycles most of the year.

Place the plants under a light fixture that will provide 20 watts of light per square foot. Keep the light source 10 to 12 inches above the top of the rose. Set the lights on a timer to establish a controlled routine of 16 to 18 hours of light per day.

There are many types of lighting fixtures and bulbs from which to choose. Many people favor the old reliable formula of equal portions of fluorescent tubes and incandescent bulbs. You may elect to use two cool white fluorescent tubes, one cool and one warm tube, or the full-spectrum fluorescents such as Agro-lite, Vita-lite, or Duro-lite, that are designed for plant growth.

Multiply your rose collection

Propagating new rose bushes from existing plants is fairly easy. Duplicating roses that you already grow saves money, and it's fun to watch the new plant emerge and develop. You can share with friends or exchange cuttings or seedlings with other rosarians in order to build up a collection of hard-to-find roses. Just be sure that any plants you reproduce are non-patented roses. See page 72.

Growing from seed

Seed propagation can be practiced with species roses, or with the new seeds resulting from hybridization (see pages 70-71).

Select a shallow tray or flat with several drainage holes; fill with fine sand or vermiculite. Shell the seed and plant ½ inch deep. Water thoroughly. Keep the sprouting medium moist, never soggy wet, and warm (around 55-60° F.). Provide no light for the first month. Then give 16 hours of light a day.

Germination will soon begin, and continue for two or three months.

Seedlings emerge with a bent neck and straighten out in a few days. Cotyledons (seed leaves) will stretch out horizontally and turn green.

They are then ready to transplant to a potting medium. American Rose Society recommends a medium composed of equal parts sterilized topsoil, perlite, and peat moss. To each bushel of the mixture add 1 cup of dolomite lime, 1 cup of superphosphate, 1 cup rose food, and 1 cup of 50% Captan.

Transplant the tiny seedlings into well-drained, large plastic or metal pans or flats filled with the growing medium. Give them 16 hours of good light per day in a warm place (70° F.). Fluorescent fixtures give excellent, controlled lighting for growing the seedlings.

Water sparingly. Blot off any water that remains on leaves. Give plenty of ventilation. After the first true leaves form, put into 3-inch pots with the same soil mixture, continue growing in flats, or transplant into the garden. Seedlings may bloom when several months old.

Seedlings that do well should be budded onto sturdy rootstock. Others may either be eliminated or recrossed with other hybrids.

Budding for vigorous growth

Budding or bud-grafting is the common propagation method for hybrid roses to give them a more vigorous root system. The technique is an inexpensive way of duplicating plants since each cane cutting (budwood) will have at least four buds, each capable of producing a new plant.

In the fall or winter, select a healthy piece of rootstock and root 8- to 10-inch cuttings, leaving only the top two buds to develop. *Rosa multiflora* and 'Dr. Huey' are the most commonly used plants; any sturdy shrub or old rose that roots easily will do.

The following spring or summer, cut a piece of budwood from the hybrid rose or new seedling. Wrap it in plastic and age in refrigerator for a few weeks. Then, using a small sharp knife, cut a scion (a single bud and a small portion of the surrounding bark) from the budwood.

Cut a T-shaped opening in the outer skin of the rooted stock cane, below the foliage. Insert the bud or scion into the T-cut on the rootstock plant. Be sure that the bud is all the way into the cut.

Bind the bud into the grafting cut with a piece of budding rubber or

This recently emerged rose seedling holds within it all the potential for many years of beautiful flowers.

Hardwood cuttings

Here's a simple way to reproduce old bush and climbing roses.

In late fall or early winter, cut mature canes of the current season's growth into 5- to 6-inch lengths. Bury them vertically in a box of sand or peat moss. Store in a cool place (32-50°F.). Keep moist through winter. The plants should be ready to put out into the garden in spring.

You can also treat them like softwood cuttings, except do not place them under a plastic cover. Keep soil medium moist and cool.

Refrigeration method for warm climates only. A successful method of propagating old roses in warm climates relies on refrigeration. Make a 5- to 6-inch cutting, wrap it in plastic, and put in refrigerator to callous. After a few weeks, pot in sand and perlite, peat moss, or a soilless medium, and put inside a plastic bag. Place the bagged pot in the refrigerator for two or three months. Then, place in filtered sunlight and begin watering.

Cut a scion from a piece of budwood.

Make a T-cut in the stem of rootstock.

Insert the hybrid bud inside rootstock.

a plastic bud cover (your County Extension Service can recommend local sources). Then, break the top of the rootstock between the bud graft and the foliage. This will encourage proper development of the bud union. The band rots after a few weeks, leaving the bud grafted onto the rootstock. Keep the soil moist and provide filtered sunlight.

By the following spring, if the grafted bud takes, you can expect healthy foliage. At that time, the greenery of the rootstock is completely removed, including any rootstock growth buds (the source of suckers). Vigorous new roots support the young plant as it continues to grow and develop.

Bind the bud onto the rootstock stem.

Remove stock top when hybrid growth starts.

Let the top two leaves remain . . .

Pull off lower leaves, being careful not to damage buds

Set cuttings into damp soil mix

Seal in a plastic bag until new shoots appear— in about 5 to 8 weeks

Transplant to a pot or planter, or its own place in your rose garden

Softwood stem cuttings

The easy way to reproduce favorite plants, especially successful with old and shrub roses.

Make 6- to 8-inch cuttings when bloom has faded. Remove the flower, along with a few inches of the top stem. Leave only one or two leaves at the top. Dip the bottom end into a root hormone stimulant to speed up root development.

Set cuttings, immersed to one-half their length, into a damp growing medium composed of equal parts sand (or perlite) and peat moss (or vermiculite).

Insert two tall stakes into the soil to support a plastic bag. Seal to create a greenhouselike climate. Store in a bright place away from direct sunlight.

Remove the bag when new growth begins (usually five to eight weeks). Transplant each cutting to a pot or to the garden where it will get partial shade for a couple of weeks.

The language of roses

Our glossary is intended to acquaint the beginning gardener who wants to learn more about roses through the terminology involved.

Bareroot. Roses dug from commercial growing fields in late winter and early spring (wrapped to preserve moisture), and shipped to retail nurseries or directly to mail-order customers.

Basal break. New cane or stem arising from the budhead tissue or bud at the base of an old cane.

Basal growth. Expanded ring of tissue at the base of a cane where it connects with the budhead or another cane.

Break. Any new growth from the buds.

Bud. Has several meanings to the rosarian. Refers to the unopened flower. Or the eyes on the cane at the nodes, base of the cane, or the budhead. The origin of all new replacement growth.

Budding. Process of propagating a new rose plant by taking a growth eye and grafting it to understock.

Budhead. Enlarged expanded growth from a single bud just above the crown where a hybrid or a different variety of rose was grafted.

Bud union. A suture line where the hybrid budhead joins the rootstock.

Canes. Main stems of the rose plant. They bear the leaves, flowers, and fruits (hips).

Candelabra. A strong, dominant cane with accelerated growth originating from the bud union, exploding into a candelabra of blooms.

Clippers. Short hand tool that cuts from both sides with either curved or straight blades.

Corky layer. Tissue which extends beyond the skin of a cane forming a thick, spongy layer over the outside of the stem.

Crown. The point where roots and stems join. Or an expanded and enlarged area which is more stem in character than root.

Cultivar. A term designating a plant that has been horticulturally derived in cultivation (by mutation, or hybridizing, or a breeding program). Distinguished from a natural variety that occurs in the wild or is grown in the garden.

Disbudding. Thinning out flower buds to develop better quality in the remaining blooms.

Dog-leg. A cane which grows outward, then upward in a deformed position.

Dormant. The period when a plant rests and its growth processes greatly slow down. Begins as days grow shorter and temperatures begin to drop. Period ends when the plant is exposed to higher temperatures for an extended number of hours.

Forked terminal. The end of a pruned cane having two smaller canes at its top, extending in opposite directions from one or more joints.

Genus. A plant classification, ranking between a family and a species. Designated by Latin or latinized and capitalized singular noun. Example: *Rosa*.

Hat-rack. Dead end or stub of a cane that has been cut between buds or above stem joints.

Hip. The fruit of the rose; a seed pod formed from pollinated flowers after the petals fade.

Hybrid. Offspring of two plants of different species or varieties.

Hybrid budhead. Growth where a hybrid variety has been budded to rootstock of a lesser variety, seedling, or species plant.

Internode. Stem space between two nodes or buds. The tissue is not regenerative in this area.

Joint. Thickened areas on canes at which buds appear and from which all replacement growth arises.

Jointed terminal. End of a pruned cane having a smaller cane attached to it by a joint and continuing away on an angle.

Leaf scar. A line extending around the cane and thickened just under the bud at the node of a stem.

Lopper. Pruning shears with extended handles at least 20 inches long.

Mulch. Any material placed on the soil to conserve soil moisture, maintain a more even temperature, and aid in weed control.

Mutation. A change in a plant gene that produces a new variety differing from the parent. Usually called a "sport."

Node. A joint or point where a branch, bud, or leaf meets the stem from which it develops.

Old roses. Many species of roses and hybrids developed prior to the introduction of hybrid teas and floribundas. Quite a few are still available from specialized rose growers.

Patented. Referring to rose varieties protected by U.S. government patent granting exclusive right for 17 years to the patent holder.

Pesticide. A substance (most often a chemical) used to control insects and rodents.

Plethora. Superabundance of small, undersized, low-quality buds found crowded on twigs at the top of a rose cane where careless bloom cutting has been practiced.

Prickle. The thorn on a rose cane.

Pruning. Cutting back or cutting off part of a rose cane for better shape and more fruitful growth.

Replacement. A cane that grows from a bud, replacing or filling the area of old or dead canes that have been removed.

Root connections. Root attachments to the crown or to larger roots.

Roots. Underground part of the plant that extends from the crown.

Rootstock. Seedling or species plant which was rooted from a cutting and on which the hybrid is budded.

Shears. Short hand tool with one cutting blade and a hook to prevent slippage.

Sinkage. The tendency of the rose plant to sink below the surface of the soil so that the crown, rootstock, and budhead are all below the soil's surface.

Species. Group of plants closely resembling each other and which interbreed freely. Designated by Latin or latinized uncapitalized noun or adjective that follows the genus name. *Rosa* (genus) *chinensis* (species).

Sport. See Mutation.

Standard. Any variety of rose plant grafted to a tall main stem. Also called tree rose.

Striations. Streaks or lines of corky tissue on old or mature canes, indicating that the blooming capacity is ended or near its end.

Stub. Remains of a cane which has been removed, leaving basal attachment to the mother cane and a short part of the original cane.

Sucker. Shoot or stem which arises from below the budhead, from the rootstock.

Systemic. A pesticide that is absorbed into the system of a plant causing the plant juice to become toxic to its enemies. Often combined with plant food.

Transverse cut. A crosswise cut made horizontal, or at right angles, to the direction of growth of a cane.

Twig. A small stem, often many-jointed, which grows laterally to a main cane of the rosebush.

Understock. The rose that supplies the rootstock onto which the hybrid is grafted.

Variety. A subgroup of plants in a species (the lowest or final classification) with similar characteristics. Each variety within a species keeps the basic character of the species, but has at least one, sometimes more, individual characteristics of its own. Man-made varieties are developed by crossbreeding different species. Tropicana and Peace are two popular varieties.

Whorl. A circular arrangement of leaves, flowers, or branches that grow from a node on a stem or cane.

Winterize. To provide protection from the cold.

Winterkill. To kill by exposure to abnormal winter conditions.

Keeping up with the roses

A good rosarian is never satisfied with the *status quo,* never rests on past accomplishments no matter how many awards are on display, never stops improving horticultural knowledge regardless of how well the garden grows.

There's a wealth of new information to sort through each year: new varieties are introduced; changes are made in pest control products; and new techniques and ideas are presented by both professional and amateur gardeners.

It can become a time-consuming job just sorting out what's beneficial to you. But the good rosarian will find the time to keep abreast of current developments. The best place to start is the American Rose Society.

American Rose Society

The American Rose Society currently boasts more than 18,000 members, mostly amateurs, making it the largest special plant society in the United States. There are more than 400 chapters, affiliated and associated local rose societies, throughout the country. The ARS has a new permanent headquarters in Shreveport, Louisiana, located on a 118-acre park known as The American Rose Center. There, the ARS is developing extensive rose gardens.

The American Rose Society lists the following services available for its members:

The monthly *American Rose* magazine is the only periodical devoted exclusively to information on the culture, use, and history of roses. A must for anyone seriously involved with roses.

The *American Rose Annual,* is a hard-bound book containing up-to-date, scientific information on roses and rose growing, plus other articles of general interest to rose lovers. Published yearly since 1916.

An extensive mail-lending library of books on roses and related horticulture is maintained, and personal information is provided on individual rose growing questions.

Cooperative research programs on rose growing problems are maintained at various colleges and experimental stations.

Two National Rose Meetings and Rose Shows are held each year. Assistance is given to district rose conferences and shows.

Schools are conducted in cooperation with the districts for training and accrediting qualified rose show judges. Rules and regulations are estabished for conducting rose shows.

Prizes and awards are granted for outstanding achievements in rose work.

The International Horticultural Congress has delegated ARS as the International Registration Authority for Roses. IRAR monthly and annual lists are published of all new roses registered with IRAR.

Hundreds of individual reports from all over the country are tabulated into an annual report of national ratings of all commercially available roses (see page 75). This *Handbook for Selecting Roses* is available to anyone at 25¢ per copy.

An annual tabulation of the cultivars winning awards at rose shows is printed.

Liaison is maintained with field societies and rosarians through strategically placed personnel called Consulting Rosarians. These individuals are available to help anyone with rose problems. A list is available from the Society.

Rose show supplies, books, program materials, and other data relative to complete operation of a rose society are available.

To start your membership in this active society send $15.50 ($12.50 if over 65) to **American Rose Society,** P.O. Box 30,000, Shreveport, LA 71130.

Cooperative Extension Service

Your County Agent or State University Cooperative Extension Service *may* offer bulletins on roses with regionalized rose-growing tips. Call your agent or write the State Extension Office to see what's available. See page 25 for your state address.

Our sampling for information turned up the following examples:

Roses in Arizona—A-30 (Arizona);

Rose Culture for Georgia Gardeners— B-671 (Georgia);

Roses: Selection and Planting— G6600 (10¢) (Missouri);

Successful Rose Culture— C200 (40¢) (North Carolina);

Roses for the Home—H & G #25 (New Hampshire);

Rose (Rosa) Disorder: Rust—A2536 (5¢) (Wisconsin).

Free information from suppliers

Catalogs and brochures on rose culture are available free of charge from many commercial rose growers and suppliers. Write for available information. See page 26 for address.

Recommended reading

Anyone Can Grow Roses
    Dr. Cynthia Wescott (Collier)
Climbing Roses
    Helen Van Pelt Wilson (M. Barrows)
History of the Rose
    Roy E. Shepherd (Macmillan)
How to Grow Roses
    Edited by Philip Edinger
    (Sunset Books)
How to Grow Roses
    L. H. D. McFarland and Robert Pyle
    (Macmillan)
Modern Roses 7
    (The McFarland Company)
Old Roses for Modern Gardens
    Richard Thomson (D. Van Nostrand)
Rockwells' Complete Book of Roses
    F. F. Rockwell and Esther C. Grayson
    (Doubleday)
Rose Recipes
    Jean Gordon (Red Rose Publications)
Rose Recipes from Olden Times
    Eleanour Sinclair Rohde
    (Dover Publications)
Roses
    James Underwood Crockett
    (Time-Life Books)
Roses for Every Garden
    R. C. Allen (M. Barrows)
Roses for Pleasure
    Richard Thomson and
    Helen Van Pelt Wilson
    (D. Van Nostrand)
Shrub Roses for Every Garden
    Michael Gibson (Collins)
The Book of Old Roses
    Dorothy Stemler
    (Bruce Humphries Publishers)
The Dictionary of Roses in Color
    S. Millar Gault and Patrick M. Synge
    (Madison Square Press)
The Magic World of Roses
    Matthew A. R. Bassity
    (Hearthside Press)
The Old Shrub Roses
    Graham Thomas (Phoenix House)
The Terrace Gardener's Handbook
    Linda Yang (Doubleday)
Wild and Old Garden Roses
    Gordon Edwards (Macmillan)
Handbook on Roses — $1.50 from
    Brooklyn Botanic Gardens
    1000 Washington Avenue
    Brooklyn, NY 11225

In search of the perfect rose

Try your hand at hybridizing to create a new rose. All you need are a few blooms, a bit of luck, and a lot of patience.

Ralph Moore, owner of Sequoia Nursery, of Visalia, California, has been a pioneer in miniature roses and certainly one of America's most prolific rose breeders.

If you check the results of the American Rose Society's annual survey to establish ratings for all the roses currently available in the United States, you'll notice that not one single rose is rated 10.0 or *Perfect.*

In fact, out of 1,250 roses listed, only two hybrid teas, one floribunda, one grandiflora, one climber, two miniatures, and two shrubs rate 9.0 or above, which is classed *Outstanding.* (See rating scale and list of top roses on page 75.)

Today's roses are the result of centuries of genetic reshuffling—the work of both nature and man. The hybridizers have been able to combine and recombine genes for constant improvement. New colors, forms, textures, habits, and fragrances, as well as more vigor and disease resistance have resulted from man's attempt to reach perfection.

But there is still a large degree of luck involved. Nature remains boss and occasionally reminds us by producing something totally new or unexpected.

Most of the roses currently on the world's market have been produced by

◁

Nature's own hybridizer at work on the pollen of hybrid tea Futura. Home gardeners can learn to do the same within controlled experiments.

the work of about 50 professional hybridizers. Each one cross-pollinates thousands of roses per year in hopes of finding that "perfect" one. The number of possible genetic combinations for new roses is mind-boggling, but the odds have been placed at about 10,000 to 1 against any specific cross-fertilization producing an outstanding new rose.

Developments in roses are not left in the hands of the professionals. These 50 or so rosarians are joined by numerous amateurs, some of whom are lucky enough to come up with a good rose—one that becomes a commercial success, and even an award winner.

Carl Meyer, a pipe fitter, experimented for 7 years before coming up with what he considered a worthy seedling. Then, after 4 more years of testing, the rose was released by Star Roses as Portrait. The rose underwent still another 2 years of tests before it was named All-America Rose Selection in 1972.

Perhaps the "perfect" rose will never be recognized. After all, perfection is an elusive quality. What may be most desirable in a rose to one person, may be unappreciated by another. Still the search continues.

The trick is being able to recognize something worth developing when it comes up. Does it have something

unique to offer? Are there qualities in color, form, or fragrance that make your rose superior to others? Maybe the "perfect" rose has been discarded in someone's greenhouse as an unworthy candidate.

Your chance to join in the search for the perfect rose is as close as your rose garden . . . to begin is as simple as the steps outlined on the next two pages.

Bill Warriner, Director of Plant Research at Jackson and Perkins, Tustin, California, has developed three All-America winners—Medallion, Bon-Bon, and Seashell.

How to create a new rose

All roses are bisexual—nature has provided each rose with both stamens (male organs) and pistils (female organs) for self-pollination. In simplest terms, roses are hybridized by taking the pollen from the stamens on the flower of one plant and applying it to the pistils on the flower of another. The process begins early in the rose season to allow plenty of time for the complete cycle to take place before dormancy sets in again.

The parental role depends on whether a rose is chosen to *provide* the pollen or *receive* it. It seems to be a tossup as to which parent has the greatest influence in transmitting its characteristics. So the experts make reciprocal crossings, using the same variety as both male and female.

If you carefully remove the flower petals from a rose you will find both sets of reproductive organs. The very center contains the pistils, delicate stalks that are connected to an ovary at the bottom end and a pollen-receiving stigma at the tip.

Surrounding the pistils are the stamens, slender stalks tipped by the anthers—kernel-like sacs which hold the pollen. The first phase of hybridization is to emasculate both parents. Even if a particular rose is being used as a female, the anthers must be removed before they have a chance to open and self-pollinate the rose. Remove the petals from partially opened buds, and pluck the anthers off with tweezers or cut them with a sharp knife, being careful not to damage the pistils.

Place the anthers gathered from the rose chosen to be the male to dry in a closed jar, dated and identified according to variety. The flower that furnished the pollen may be discarded, or used as a female in a simultaneous experiment.

In a day or so the anthers inside the jar will ripen and open (dehisce), releasing their dustlike pollen grains. These are actually minute capsules containing the sperm.

During this time the female parent prepares to receive the pollen. When the female's stigmas are tipped with a sticky secretion, it is time for the pollination.

Brush all of the dry pollen onto the receptive stigmas with an artist's camelhair brush. The secretion of the stigma not only makes the pollen adhere, but also dissolves the capsule, releasing the tiny sperm. The sperm

1. *Remove the outer petals of selected parents to expose the flower's reproductive organs.*

2. *In the center are pistils, surrounded by stamens that are tipped with pollen-bearing anthers.*

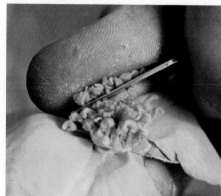

3. *Remove the anthers from both parents before they ripen, open, and self-pollinate the rose.*

4. *Store anthers from the chosen male inside a labeled container and allow to dry.*

5. *In about a day a sticky secretion appears on the stigma as an indication it is pollen-receptive.*

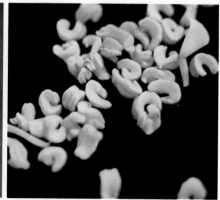

6. *At about the same time, the anthers release their dustlike pollen grains containing the sperm.*

7. *Using a small, soft brush, place the dried pollen onto the female's sticky-coated stigma.*

8. *Label the pollinated bud and cover it with a glassine bag for protection against dust and unwanted pollen.*

9. *If pollination is successful, the hip will swell with growth as in the fertile hip on the right.*

10. *Sometimes seeds are borne on the outside of the hip. Harvest about 2½ months after the crossing.*

11. *When the hip has matured and turned color, cut it carefully with a small sharp knife.*

12. *Divide the hip into sections and peel them open to reveal the seeds that have developed.*

13. *Stratify the seeds by placing them in peat moss and storing at 40° F. for up to six weeks.*

14. *Plant seeds in a very loose growing medium or wait for germination. This seedling is one week old.*

15. *Evaluate the results of your cross and weed out seedlings that are weak or have poor color.*

16. *Label the most promising seedlings for continued development and budding at the end of summer.*

then sends down tiny, hairlike pollen tubes through the stalks to an ovule containing unfertilized eggs. There, a male reproductive cell seeks out and unites with an egg.

After the crossing is complete, label the female flower to identify the variety that served as the male parent. Tie a bag (paper, glassine, or plastic) over the flower to protect it from dust or unwanted pollen. Now it's up to nature. Don't be disappointed with failure. The percentage of fertilizations is low.

The hip will dry up and fall off the plant if the pollination fails to take. On those that take, the hip will stay green, and within a few weeks will swell with growth.

The seed hips ripen in about 2½ months, turning bright orange, yellow, red, or brown, depending upon variety or species. Gather the hips (along with the label) when they first turn color, before they become overripe. Fresh seed tend to germinate faster.

Next, slice the hip carefully with a knife, expose the seeds, and remove them. There may be only one seed or as many as 50.

Condition (stratify) the seeds by storing them in polyethylene bags of peat moss. Refrigerate at 40° F. for about six weeks.

When you remove the seeds from refrigeration, plant them according to the seed propagation procedure outlined on page 64.

The first flowers may appear seven to eight weeks after germination. This is the first indication of your results. Now you must make the decision, according to your personal preference, whether the seedling merits being left to develop for further testing or if it should be discarded.

At the end of summer, a seedling will be ready to be budded onto rootstock for extensive testing, propagation, and evaluation (see pages 64-65).

If you think you've come up with the perfect rose—or at least a good one—send one of your seedlings to a respected commercial rose grower. Be sure and correspond with him prior to shipping your plant. (See catalog listing, page 26.) He will evaluate your results and possibly purchase the rights for development and distribution. Of course, you can just grow the rose for your own pleasure.

You may benefit from membership in the Rose Hybridizers Association. For details, write to Mr. Pete Haring, Fox Hill Lane, Box 35, Stony Brook, NY 11790.

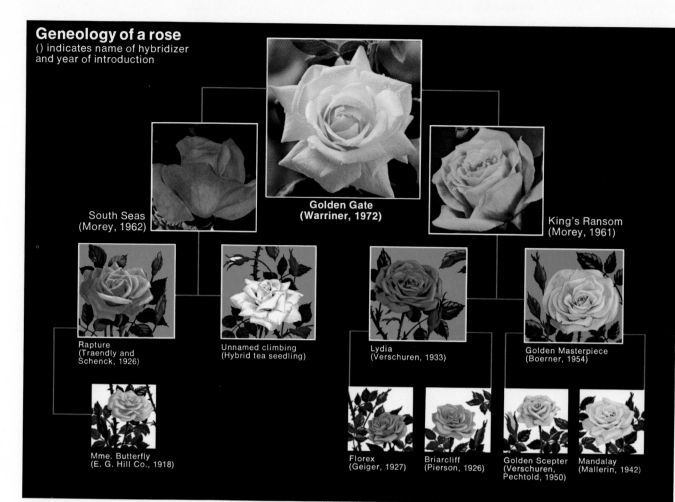

Geneology of a rose
() indicates name of hybridizer and year of introduction

Golden Gate
(Warriner, 1972)

South Seas
(Morey, 1962)

King's Ransom
(Morey, 1961)

Rapture
(Traendly and Schenck, 1926)

Unnamed climbing
(Hybrid tea seedling)

Lydia
(Verschuren, 1933)

Golden Masterpiece
(Boerner, 1954)

Mme. Butterfly
(E. G. Hill Co., 1918)

Florex
(Geiger, 1927)

Briarcliff
(Pierson, 1926)

Golden Scepter
(Verschuren, Pechtold, 1950)

Mandalay
(Mallerin, 1942)

The testing period

A rose hybridizer must be patient. It may take ten years or more from the birth of a new rose to its official public introduction. Once a successful breeding is completed, the rose becomes merely a number in the test garden of a commercial rose grower. There, it will be submitted to a rigorous testing program.

A typical rose company examines seedlings of as many as 600 different new roses per year. Ninety-five percent of these originate within the company, or with professional hybridizers. From these seedlings about 25 to 30 will be deemed worthy of further observation. Out of these, a dozen or so will be retained for more trials, and may be grown for as long as five years. After this, only four or five will be lucky enough to be chosen for public introduction.

Protecting your investment

Up until the 1930 passage of the Townsend-Purnell Act, a hybridizer could go through the process of developing a new rose and never reap any financial benefits. As soon as a plant was released, it could be immediately propagated by anyone.

Today the Plant Patent Act protects the inventor of plants in the same way that industrial inventions are protected.

"Whoever invents or discovers and asexually reproduces any distinct and new variety of plant, including cultivated sports, mutants, hybrids, and newly formed seedlings . . . may obtain a patent therefore subject to the conditions and requirements of this title."

The patent owner is given legal protection for 17 years. During that time the owner receives a royalty for every offspring of his plant. This gives a chance to recoup the investment cost, and maybe even show a profit for all the efforts. Commercial rose nurseries can purchase the patent rights from the inventor and receive enough return to compensate for the expensive publicity necessary to introduce the new rose.

All patented roses are required to have a metal tag attached. This is your guarantee of the plant variety and quality. Avoid buying roses sold as "patented" unless they wear this identification tag with patent number.

During these years of testing, the roses are judged for petal count, color, fragrance, foliage, disease resistance, and other factors important to the rosarian.

Since roses introduced to the public represent considerable investment in growing space, time, labor, and promotion, the commercial rose nurseries must select those that will do well nationally under various extremes.

In addition to their own test gardens, reliable rose companies rely on test panels or test gardens throughout the country to field test the roses being considered. In checking through the results of one company, we noted the following comments on why certain roses were dropped from further testing:

"C65-8031: Although this rose seemed to have great merit in our test gardens, nationwide tests indicated that its cycle between blooming periods was too long . . .

"66-11533: Plant made poor comeback after first bloom . . .

"C66-7591: Awkward habit . . .

"C64-5182: Proved to be nonvigorous in many regions. The color, although pleasing, faded too quickly in many climates . . .

"C63-3937: Geographical variance in plant performance and disease resistance . . .

"58-6103: Unstable color . . ."

What's in a name?

Once a rose is ready for its public debut, it will need a name. The hybridizer or distributing nursery registers the name with the American Rose Society, which has been designated as our National Rose Registration Center by the International Registration Authority for Roses.

The registration center reviews the chosen name, which is accompanied by complete descriptions, and rejects names that do not conform to provisions of the International Code. Non-acceptable names include those that are too similar to existing roses. It is possible to reuse a name after 30 years, if proof can be supplied that the original rose is extinct, not of historical importance, or was not used as a parent of an existing cultivar.

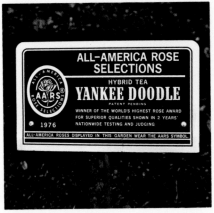

AARS signs are proudly displayed in public rose gardens.

All-America Rose Selections

Unfortunately the Plant Patent Act only requires that a plant be different in some respect from existing plants. Within a short time, after 1930, patents were granted to many roses of inferior quality and performance. The public was paying a higher price for merchandise of questionable quality.

Rose people knew something had to be done to test the merits of new roses before they were offered to the public. In 1938, All-America Rose Selections was born. The nonprofit organization tests new rose originations, gives recognition in the form of an All-America award to the new rose candidates which have proved outstanding in two-year trials, and acquaints the press and gardening public of the United States and Canada with the award-winning roses.

AARS has been effective and has earned the confidence of the buying public—40% of the total sales of roses today are All-America winners. And in a recent poll of the American public to pick our favorite rose, all 10 of the finalists were former All-America winners. Incidentally, America's favorite rose was First Prize, followed closely by Peace.

There are 26 official AARS Test Gardens scattered in 19 states throughout the nation. Most are located at universities or large public rose gardens. They are rigidly maintained by AARS standards.

Anyone may enter the All-America competition by paying an entry fee and furnishing trial plants for the gardens. The roses are subjected to two years of testing by well-trained judges. Only cultivars scoring in first or second place in their classes are even considered by the membership for the coveted awards.

Roses that are not winners, but receive high scores, are normally introduced anyway by the firms submitting them. Those with relatively low scores are usually dropped. In this way the total number of varieties introduced is not only greatly reduced, but the quality of new cultivars marketed is higher than in the past.

All-America Winners:

Winners

1940
Dickson's Red (HT)
*Flash (Cl, HT)
*The Chief (HT)
World's Fair (F)
1941
*Apricot Queen (HT)
*California (HT)
Charlotte Armstrong (HT)
1942
Heart's Desire (HT)
1943
*Grand Duchesse Charlotte (HT)
Mary Margaret McBride (HT)
1944
†Fred Edmunds (HT)
Katherine T. Marshall (HT)
Lowell Thomas (HT)
*Mme. Chiang Kai-Shek (HT)
*Mme. Marie Curie (HT)
1945
Floradora (F)
*Horace McFarland (HT)
Mirandy (HT)
1946
Peace (HT)
1947
Rubaiyat (HT)
1948
Diamond Jubilee (HT)
†High Noon (Cl, HT)
Nocturne (HT)
Pinkie (F)
*San Fernando (HT)
Taffeta (HT)
1949
Forty-Niner (HT)
*Tallyho (HT)
1950
Capistrano (HT)
Fashion (F)
*Mission Bells (HT)
Sutter's Gold (HT)
1951
None of the 1951 Introductions were equal to the rigid AARS standards.

1952
*Fred Howard (HT)
Helen Traubel (HT)
Vogue (F)
1953
Chrysler Imperial (HT)
Ma Perkins (F)
1954
*Lilibet (F)
Mojave (HT)
1955
Jiminy Cricket (F)
Queen Elizabeth (G)
Tiffany (HT)
1956
Circus (F)
1957
Golden Showers (Cl)
White Bouquet (F)
1958
Fusilier (F)
Gold Cup (F)
White Knight (HT)
1959
Ivory Fashion (F)
Starfire (G)
1960
Fire King (F)
Garden Party (HT)
Sarabande (F)
1961
Duet (HT)
Pink Parfait (G)
1962
Christian Dior (HT)
Golden Slippers (F)
John S. Armstrong (G)
King's Ransom (HT)
1963
Royal Highness (HT)
Tropicana (HT)
1964
Granada (HT)
Saratoga (F)
1965
Camelot (G)
Mister Lincoln (HT)
1966
American Heritage (HT)
Apricot Nectar (F)
Matterhorn (HT)
1967
Bewitched (HT)
Gay Princess (F)
Lucky Lady (G)
Roman Holiday (F)

1968
Europeana (F)
Miss All-American Beauty (HT)
Scarlet Knight (G)
1969
Angel Face (F)
Comanche (G)
Gene Boerner (F)
Pascali (HT)
1970
First Prize (HT)
1971
Aquarius (G)
Command Performance (HT)
Redgold (F)
1972
Apollo (HT)
Portrait (HT)
1973
Electron (HT)
Gypsy (HT)
Medallion (HT)
1974
Bahia (F)
Bon-Bon (F)
Perfume Delight (HT)
1975
Arizona (G)
Oregold (HT)
Rose Parade (F)
1976
America (Cl)
Cathedral (F)
Seashell (F)
Yankee Doodle (HT)
1977
First Edition (F)
Double Delight (HT)
Prominent (G)

Note: For annual additions, write All-America Rose Selections, P.O. Box 218, Shenandoah, IA 51601.

Cl — *Climbing*

F — *Floribunda*

G — *Grandiflora*

HT — *Hybrid tea*

†Denotes regional recommendation.

*No longer generally available.

These four famous All-America Selections were still top-rated in 1976 national testing by American Rose Society: (Clockwise from top) First Prize, AARS 1970; Peace, AARS 1946; Queen Elizabeth, AARS 1955 (all three rated 9.0); and Tiffany, AARS 1955 (rated 8.8).

Other awards for roses

Although the AARS brings the most prestige to a new rose, and the most financial return, there are a number of other prestigious awards given to well-tested roses. These include:

Bagatelle Gold Medal (Paris)
Geneva Gold Medal
Madrid Gold Medal
Portland (Oregon) Gold Medal
Rome Gold Medal
Royal National Rose Society of
    Great Britain Gold Medal
The Hague Gold Medal and
    Golden Rose

Also included are a number of awards given by the American Rose Society, including the National Gold Medal Certificate.

There's even a special award for rose fragrance. The James Alexander Gamble Rose Fragrance Medal is granted by the American Rose Foundation. Through 1976, only six roses had been honored with this award:

Crimson Glory (1961)
Tiffany (1962)
Chrysler Imperial (1965)
Sutter's Gold (1966)
Granada (1968)
Fragrant Cloud (1970)

Winners of ARS National Gold Medal Certificates

Peace (1948)
City of York (1950)
Carrousel (1954)
Fashion (1954)
Frensham (1955)
Vogue (1956)
Chrysler Imperial (1956)
Golden Wings (1958)
Queen Elizabeth (1960)
Montezuma (1961)
Spartan (1961)
Toy Clown (1966)
Tropicana (1967)

The proof of the pudding

Probably one of the most meaningful tests of roses is the national survey taken each year by the ARS to determine the quality of roses grown by its members in their home gardens. These ratings, called "Proof of the Pudding," are based on the gardening experiences and opinions of a great number of the members of American Rose Society who have actually grown the roses in question.

Roses remain on the checklist for three years to establish a rating. Comments and opinions are sent to district reporters throughout the country. They compile the results and send their findings to ARS. The final tabulation is a composite of reports from all parts of the nation.

You can keep abreast of new additions or yearly changes in the ratings by annually ordering a copy of the Handbook for Selecting Roses from American Rose Society, Box 30,000, Shreveport, LA 71130, at a cost of 25¢.

Here we list the roses that were rated at least 8.0 in the 1976 Handbook. Note the large number of old roses and shrubs that stay right up there with the new cultivars. It's also interesting to see that the highest rated rose is a miniature, Starina.

National rating scale:

10.0	Perfect
9.9 - 9.0	Outstanding
8.9 - 8.0	Excellent
7.9 - 7.0	Good
6.9 - 6.0	Fair
5.9 and lower	Of questionable value

Highest-rated roses

Climbers
Hoosier Beauty 9.0
Galway Bay 8.7
Don Juan 8.6
Handel 8.6
Kitty Kininmonth 8.5
May Queen 8.4
Casa Blanca 8.1
Lawrence Johnston 8.0
Sunday Best 8.0

Floribunda
CoralGlo 9.0
Europeana 8.8
Little Darling 8.8
Iceberg 8.6
Walko 8.5
Gene Boerner 8.4
Sea Pearl 8.4
Betty Prior 8.3
Lichterloh 8.3
City of Belfast 8.2
Ginger 8.2
Sweet Vivien 8.2
Anna Wheatcroft 8.1
Evening Star 8.1
Ivory Fashion 8.1
Orange Sensation 8.1
Sarabande 8.1
Angel Face 8.0
Chuckles 8.0
City of Leeds 8.0
Orangeade 8.0
Paris Red 8.0

Grandiflora
Queen Elizabeth 9.0
Pink Parfait 8.4

Hybrid tea
First Prize 9.0
Peace 9.0
Granada 8.8
Tiffany 8.8
Tropicana 8.8
Mister Lincoln 8.7
Garden Party 8.6
Fragrant Cloud 8.5
Century Two 8.4
Dainty Bess 8.4
Lady X 8.4
Royal Highness 8.4
Swarthmore 8.4
Chicago Peace 8.3
Chrysler Imperial 8.3
Miss All-American
    Beauty 8.3
Big Ben 8.2
Duet 8.2
George Dickson 8.2
Kentucky Derby 8.2

Confidence 8.1
Alec's Red 8.0
Electron 8.0
Pascali 8.0
Wini Edmunds 8.0

Miniatures
Starina 9.4
Beauty Secret 9.0
Cinderella 8.9
Toy Clown 8.9
Judy Fischer 8.8
Mary Marshall 8.7
Magic Carrousel 8.6
Simplex 8.6
Starglo 8.6
Chipper 8.5
Over the Rainbow 8.5
Kathy 8.4
Peachy 8.4
Pink Cameo 8.4
Baby Darling 8.3
Hi Ho 8.3
Janna 8.3
Jeanie Williams 8.3
Kara 8.3
Scarlet Gem 8.3
Sheri Anne 8.3
White Angel 8.3
Willie Winkie 8.3
Yellow Doll 8.3
Opal Jewel 8.2
Pixie Rose 8.2
Rosmarin 8.2
Baby Betsy McCall 8.1
Dwarfking 8.1
Robin 8.1
Top Secret 8.1
Easter Morning 8.0
Mary Adair 8.0

Old Garden Roses
Duchesse de Montebello
    (G) 9.0
Jeannette (G) 8.8
Mme. Hardy (D) 8.7
Mme. Plantier (D) 8.6
R. gallica officinalis
    (G) 8.6
Frühlingsgold (HSpn)
    8.4
Henri Martin (M) 8.4
Mme. Alfred Carrière (N)
    8.4
R. rubrifolia 8.4
Sombreuil (T) 8.4
Paul's Early Blush (HP)
    8.3
Tuscany (G) 8.3
Félicité Parmentier (A)
    8.2

R. damascena bifera (D)
    8.2
Vierge de Cléry (C) 8.2
Mme. Legras de
    St. Germain (A) 8.1
Captain Hayward (HP) 8.0
Koenigin von
    Daenemark (A) 8.0
R. hugonis 8.0

A — *Alba*
C — *Centifolia*
D — *Damask*
G — *Gallica*
HP — *Hybrid Perpetual*
HSpn — *Hybrid*
    Spinosissima
M — *Moss*
N — *Noisette*
T — *Tea*

Polyanthas
The Fairy 8.4
Dopey 8.0

Shrub
Country Dancer 9.3
Eddie's Crimson (HM) 9.1
R. rugosa rubra 8.8
Hanseat 8.7
Square Dancer 8.7
Wanderin' Wind 8.7
Will Alderman (HRg) 8.7
Dortmund (K) 8.6
Lillian Gibson (HBla) 8.6
Prairie Princess 8.5
Alchymist 8.4
Golden Wings 8.4
R. rugosa alba 8.4
Rosaleen (HMsk) 8.4
Fresh Pink 8.2
Saabrücken 8.2
Belinda (HMsk) 8.1
Berlin 8.1
Frau Dagmar Hartopp
    (HRg) 8.1
Nevada (HM) 8.1
Sea Foam 8.1
Applejack 8.0
Blanc Double de
    Coubert (HRg) 8.0
Cerise Bouquet 8.0
Conrad O'Neal 8.0
Roseraie de l'Hay
    (HRg) 8.0
Weisse aus
    Sparrieshoop 8.0

HBla — *Hybrid Blanda*
HM — *Hybrid Moyesii*
HMsk — *Hybrid Musk*
HRg — *Hybrid Rugosa*
K — *Kordesii*

Enjoying cut roses

Whether you choose one lovely bloom in a bud vase or a basket of mixed varieties, roses can add beauty, color, and fragrance to your interior environment.

Legend has it that Cleopatra once filled a room knee-deep in roses to welcome Marc Anthony. We know that the Romans imported shiploads of roses to make garlands and bouquets for festive occasions. It is recorded that Nero once lavished so many roses on his banquet guests that several people suffocated underneath the great piles of petals.

Today you can enjoy cut roses 12 months a year—your own garden flowers in season, and commercially grown blooms at any time.

When you cut roses from the garden, choose blooms that are only partly opened. Studies indicate that flowers cut in the late afternoon last longest. Don't cut more stem and foliage than you need. Plants need abundant leaf supply if they are to stay productive.

It's a good idea to carry a bucket of water with you to the garden.

Cut the rose with a sharp knife or shears, at an angle, and place it immediately in the water. Cut at a point where a 5-leaflet leaf appears on the stem (see pruning, pages 55-59). Allow at least two leaves to remain between the cut and the main stem. When you've finished gathering the bouquet, wash away any soil or leaf spray residue from the foliage.

Whether your cut roses come from the garden or the florist, the following tips will increase their life span. It's a temptation to place them in a vase for immediate enjoyment, but you'll have the roses around a lot longer if you take the time to prepare them properly.

Remove thorns and foliage that will be below the water level in your vase. You'll find that the water will remain sweet-smelling and have a minimum of bacteria.

◁

A "hedge" of fully opened yellow roses seems to grow from a bed of polished black Japanese river stones inside a glass building block.

The easy way to remove foliage is to take several layers of paper towel or cloth, wrap around the stem where you wish to begin removal, and pull downward to the end of the stem, stripping away thorns and leaves as you pull. Never scrape the stem with a knife. The resulting injuries shorten the life of the flowers. If the rose has only a few leaves and thorns, simply break them off with your fingers. Be careful, rose thorns can hurt.

Give the rose a fresh cut at least ½-inch above the end of the stem. Cut with a sharp knife at a sharp angle in order to expose as much cut surface to the water as possible.

Immerse the stems in deep water that is too hot for your hand (about 90° to 100° F.). Leave the roses alone until the water cools, then place the entire container in the refrigerator or a cool place for a couple of hours to condition the blooms. (Wilted roses can usually be revived by giving them a fresh cut and subjecting them to this hot sauna treatment.)

When you are ready to arrange the roses, fill a vase with fresh water, and add one of the floral preservatives (from flower shops or garden stores), carefully following manufacturer's directions. Using too much will put the roses into irreparable shock.

Arrange the flowers any way you like, giving each one a fresh slanted cut before you place it. Keep the finished bouquet in as cool a place as possible, away from drafts. Add enough fresh water daily to keep the stems immersed to one-half or two-thirds of their length. Better yet, change the water every day, adding new preservative each time. The flowers will last longer if you recut the bottom of the stem every day or so.

If you use florist's foam for arranging, soak it thoroughly in fresh water to which floral preservative has been added. Do not move the stem after you place it in the foam because air pockets will form at the base of the stem, cutting off the water supply. Keep the container filled with plenty of fresh water.

In addition to lending beauty to the interior environment, flowers gently remind us of our link with all living things. They provide a quiet, inner celebration of nature when we view them. Cut blooms add tranquility to any room. Live plants are dependent upon light for survival, but we can enjoy colorful cut roses even in the dimmest corners.

Above: Tiny miniature roses in a jam jar complement an afternoon tea tray.

Above right: A classical rose arrangement —long stemmed roses simply displayed in a clear crystal cylinder.

Right: The magic of candlelight flickering on a single red rose is captured by our photographer. The bloom floats atop a leaf of rose-scented geranium in a silver bowl.

The arrangement of flowers is a very personal thing. There are people who adhere to the strict rules of floral design that came into being with the American garden clubs. These are the principles followed in the arrangement category at rose shows. Some of us prefer English-type mixed flower baskets, the simple Oriental touch, or just a lone specimen rose in a bud vase.

Nowadays, the trend is definitely toward more natural bouquets, letting the flowers speak for themselves without imposing rigid lines or contrived forms. In any case, don't just imitate—create, and express your own personal feelings for the roses.

◊

An antique Choctaw Indian basket holds a flower garden featuring roses mixed with lilies, iris, flowering cherry, calendulas, miniature carnations, freesias, wax flower, ranunculus, stock, exotic protea, and ivy.

Above: The bamboo mirror reflects Christmas bouquets of white roses and oriental asparagus plumes in a pair of green satin glass decanters, vintage 1930.
Left: Three tiny Tiffany crystal bottles show off blooms of miniatures June Time, Fire Princess, and Lavender Lace.

Choose containers that fit the mood of the room or the occasion. Select a vase that relates visually in size with the blooms. Gleaming silver or other metal reflects the beauty of roses. Wicker baskets are good choices for garden-fresh casual bouquets, while china, porcelain, or ceramic containers are best suited to more formal arrangements. Clear glass or crystal allows you to enjoy the entire rose from the stem up. This look is most successful without the use of mechanical holders or florist's foam.

Roses are beautiful alone, or with several varieties mixed together. And they blend successfully with other garden flowers. Nothing beats rose foliage for greens, but you might try adding camellia, ivy, or rose-scented geranium leaves.

All flower bouquets in this chapter are by the author/editor, who was a horticultural designer in New York City for several years.

An Aalto freeform vase displays a profusion of pastel roses in a cool setting for a summer luncheon.

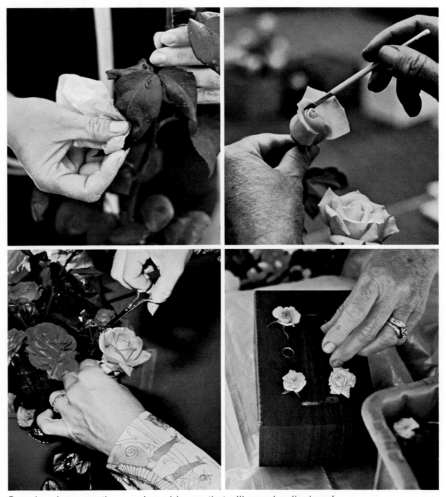

*Rose show exhibitors arrive early
to prepare for the big event.*

*Busy hands groom the specimen blooms that will soon be displayed,
first for the judges, then for the public.*

Showing prize roses

Growing prize-winning blooms is a skillful art that requires continual practice. There's a lot of work, and a good bit of luck involved in growing a rose that reaches its most beautiful phase just in time for a rose show. It takes preparation well in advance, with disbudding at just the right time to create large flowers, and extra protection from the elements, insects, and diseases.

Rose shows begin at the local level. Then there are district shows, and two annual national competitions sponsored by the American Rose Society. Check your local newspaper gardening news or calendar of events for nearby shows. Or write to ARS for complete information on rose shows. (See page 67 for address.)

Competition is steep. Judging is based on a point system: Color—25, Form—25, Substance—20, Stem and foliage—20, and Size—10. All judges must be trained and accredited by the ARS. Winners in various categories are awarded ribbons, certificates, medals, trophies, and other appropriate prizes.

Whether you want to grow exhibition roses for competition or your own enjoyment, you can learn a lot from studying the entries and winners at a rose show.

Right: Blooms are displayed together by classification. Identification tags are folded to hide entrant's name until after the judging.

Far right: Winning roses are displayed in a special area along with their prizes. Here's the King of Miniatures.

◁

A living room "rose show" featuring all the varieties from the garden grouped together in a collection of glass cylinders.

Preserving the last rose of summer

Here's a selection of old-fashioned ways, and maybe even a few new ones, of preserving some of your flowers or hips in the form of decorative accessories, fragrances, cosmetics, foods and drinks.

Drying rose blooms
Space roses about one inch apart. Hold petals with a stick as you pour in the drying medium.

Use a closed cookie tin or coffee can for drying in silica gel. Seal the lid edge with masking tape

Label each container with the sealing date and kind of flower

Align the short wire with a long, straight piece of heavy-duty florist's wire and wrap it tightly with floral tape, stretching as you go

When drying time is over pour drying medium off carefully—pull each flower free with its wire as it emerges from the sand or silica gel

---

According to mythology, the gods showered the rose with gifts when it was created. Dionysus gave the rose its nectar and fragrance. Later, the pharoahs of Egypt supervised the bottling of this fragrance, creating the first rose potpourri.

In typical excessive fashion, the Romans stuffed themselves on delicacies made of rose petals, while wine of roses flowed freely.

A Persian caliph interrupted his wedding festivities to bottle some of the oil of roses he discovered floating on petal-strewn waters; and one of Persia's major industries was born. When the Arabs conquered Persia they became enamored of roses, and rose water became a major flavoring in Arabian cookery.

American colonial women turned rose petals into a plastic substance and fashioned it into jewelry.

The desire to continue enjoying roses after the gardening season has passed is nothing new; maybe only your reasons are different.

Perhaps it's because you're sentimental. Maybe you just hate to waste anything; and enjoy finding ways to

Dried roses make beautiful winter bouquets, or they may be turned into fragrant candles or potpourris.

use everything. Whatever the reason, it's possible to continue enjoying those beautiful roses long after the flowers in the garden have faded into memory.

They are fun for the family and make delightful gifts for friends with whom you'd like to share part of your garden.

Dry roses for lasting beauty

If you've never tried drying roses you'll find that it's easy work, and highly rewarding because of the lasting pleasure the flowers provide. You can settle for one or two roses or dry a lot of them for bouquets or arrangements. And the relatively low cost will add to your enjoyment.

One easy way to dry roses is simply to tie the stems together and hang them upside down in a warm, dry place. If there's a lot of dust, wrap them gently in cheesecloth. The only problem with this method is that most of the color is lost.

Better results are achieved by drying flowers completely immersed in a desiccant, which gradually withdraws all the moisture from the flower. Small rosebuds or blooms with only a few petals dry most successfully. The flowers will last indefinitely and

can be used in winter bouquets and holiday decorations over and over again.

Expect reds and other deep colors to darken, with pinks and yellows fading slightly, although some light-colored blooms will retain much of their natural color for several seasons.

Gather roses in the morning after the dew has dried. Cut off stems and replace with a short piece of florist's wire through the heel of the rose.

Types of desiccants. Craft or hobby stores, as well as garden centers, sell several commercial preparations for drying flowers. However, the following drugstore or hardware materials seem to work equally well: household borax powder; fine-grained builder's sand (or beach sand washed in a bucket of detergent and rinsed several times); equal parts cornmeal and household borax; ground or crushed silica gel crystals (dried between uses by spreading on a cookie sheet in a low oven until blue crystals that have turned white with moisture return to their original blue.)

Method. Select an airtight container such as a large coffee can or plastic food storage box. Pour a layer of the desiccant you've chosen over the bottom of the container. Place the flower upright on top, bending the wire flat. Hold the bottom of the flower with your fingers while slowly adding more desiccant around it.

Be sure to work the material in between and completely around *every* petal. Any air pockets can invite mildew. Use a small artist's paintbrush to push lightweight materials such as borax into cavities. You'll need a little patience.

Add as many flowers as the container will hold, with none of the blooms touching each other. After the last flower is in place, cover with two more inches of the desiccant material. If using sand, leave the container uncovered. For all other materials, seal tightly. Use tape to hold the lid in place if it isn't airtight.

Carefully place the container in a warm, dry area where it can remain undisturbed until the roses are dried. Most blooms in borax or silica gel require two to three days. In sand they will take one to three weeks.

If you don't have a warm, dry place to store the container, or if you're in a hurry, place the container in an unlighted gas oven. The pilot light will keep it warm and dry, or use an electric warming oven at 150° F. Be sure to use metal containers if you choose oven drying. It is not necessary to seal the container. Sand will dry the blooms in a few days; silica gel or borax in about 10 to 15 hours. Some of the bloom's color clarity is lost with the fast method.

To test readiness in any of the methods above, gently remove a flower from the container. It should feel dry, crisp, and make a rustling sound when you touch it. If not completely dry, return to the box and cover completely once again. Test the following day (or in a few hours if using the oven method).

When the flowers are dry, carefully remove from the container, hold upside down and gently shake off the desiccant. Again use your small brush to remove any material that clings to the bloom.

Store the completed flowers in a dry room away from direct sunlight until ready to use. To make stems longer, add any desired length of florist's wire and wrap with florist tape, stretching it as you go.

Hips for winter decoration

Colorful clusters of rose hip fruits are attractive in arrangements, as package decorations, on holiday trees or wreaths, and for other imaginative uses. Their bright color will fade slightly to deep orange when dried in the following manner.

Mix one part glycerin (from your pharmacy) to two parts very hot water in a tightly closed bottle. Shake well to thoroughly mix. Pour into a saucepan and bring to boiling point.

Place clusters of rose hips in a container and pour in the glycerin mixture so the solution will reach about two inches up the stems.

It normally takes two to three weeks for rose hips to become preserved. They should be soft and shiny after the water and glycerin have been absorbed by every part of the plant material. The water evaporates and leaves the glycerin behind in the cells, preserving the hips indefinitely.

Check regularly to see that the hips do not absorb all the solution before preservation is complete. If the solution is gone, pour in more hot water (not boiling this time) up to the original level.

If beads of moisture appear on the surface of the fruit, then they have been in solution longer than necessary and cannot absorb any more. Remove from the solution and wipe off the excess moisture.

Before storing or using the preserved hips, spray lightly with hair lacquer. Keep in a cool, dry room to retain suppleness.

Pressed petals and leaves

Almost everyone remembers pressing flowers as a school science project. Usually the blooms are placed between sheets of newsprint or blotting paper, inserted between pages of a large heavy book, and weighted down with several other books until the petals have dried.

Here's a slightly more sophisticated method of utilizing a flower press for those who want to keep a few of the petals and leaves from their roses to turn into pictures, notecards, or other personal remembrances.

You can buy a flower press in a hobby or toy store, but it's more fun to make your own. Simply cut two 1-foot squares of plywood. Drill holes one inch from each corner. Cut several pieces of corrugated cardboard and sheets of blotting paper to fit inside, cutting off the corners to allow room for screws to pass.

Stack layers of cardboard, blotting paper, petals or leaves, more blotting paper and cardboard. Continue alternating layers until press is filled (make sure the petals are not touching when you lay them on the blotting paper).

Insert 3- to 4-inch screws and fasten tightly with wing nuts (see diagram).

Store the press in a warm, dry place for at least four weeks. The longer the petals are pressed initially, the better they will retain color.

When you are ready to use the flowers, unscrew the press, remove sheets and carefully lift off petals and leaves with tweezers. If you must keep them for a while before making a design, store them between tissue sheets in envelopes in a warm, dry place to keep them from absorbing moisture.

Press many kinds of flowers and leaves so you'll have a good selection for your creations.

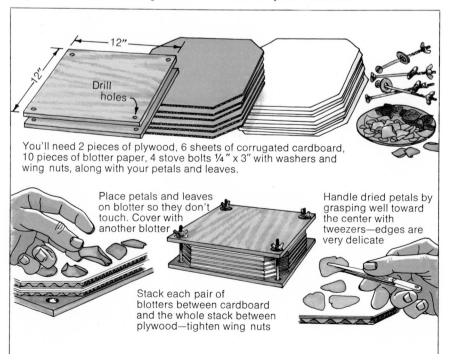

You'll need 2 pieces of plywood, 6 sheets of corrugated cardboard, 10 pieces of blotter paper, 4 stove bolts ¼" x 3" with washers and wing nuts, along with your petals and leaves.

Place petals and leaves on blotter so they don't touch. Cover with another blotter

Stack each pair of blotters between cardboard and the whole stack between plywood—tighten wing nuts

Handle dried petals by grasping well toward the center with tweezers—edges are very delicate

To decorate cards, form your design and glue petals down with thinned rubber cement. Burnish by covering with tissue paper and rubbing the surface with your fingers or a flat stick. When the glue dries, carefully rub off the excess from around edges of the petals.

If you want to create a picture with your flowers and leaves, select a suitable piece of artist's mounting board. Cut to the size you wish and lay plant material down to form a design. Then carefully glue each piece to the board with rubber cement as in making cards.

When the picture is complete, wrap it temporarily in blotting paper until time to frame it.

Place the picture flush to the glass of the frame to make it as airtight as possible and to prevent deterioration. Add a piece of heavy cardboard to the back and seal it to the frame with masking tape.

For a more contemporary design, glue the petals directly onto a piece of glass or lucite, cover with a duplicate sheet of glass or lucite, and clip together. These "frames" are available in many good frame shops.

To retain good color, hang flower pictures as far away from direct sunlight as possible.

Capturing the fragrance of the rose in potpourri, candles, soaps, and beads

"The rose looks fair, but fairer it we deem for that sweet odor which doth in it live." When Shakespeare wrote these words he must have had potpourri (po poo re') in mind. This pleasant old way to preserve the memories of a lovely rose garden still delights today as it has for centuries.

The custom probably originated with the pharaohs, who buried pots of roses for years. The French called the concoction "rotton pot" because the old moist method of making potpourri actually let the petals slowly rot in a jar. The jar was opened to relieve the stale atmosphere of damp, stuffy houses.

Today potpourri is usually made by the dry method, but it can still sweeten the air with its heady aroma. Draw upon your imagination for ways to package the fragrant mixture, to create unique gifts. Potpourri is a sentimental way to share the beauty and fragrance of your roses with friends.

Creating potpourri

Pick roses in the early morning after the dew is gone. The fresher the flower, the more essential oil will remain when it is dried. As to varieties, let your nose be the judge in choosing fragrances.

Cut the flowers and gently pull off the petals. Dry a few small leaves and some tiny buds each time. Dry other fragrant garden flowers (lavender, violets, freesia), leaves, and herbs at the same time and in the same way, to mix with the roses.

Select an area away from strong light, where warm air can circulate, and spread the petals, leaves, and buds on some sort of drying rack, such as a window screen. Or spread them on cheesecloth or newspaper on a tabletop or the floor. If the area is breezy, put a layer of cheesecloth over the petals. Stir or turn them daily.

The petals for moist potpourri should be dried only a few days, just until they are limp, not crispy. Flowers going into dry mixtures should be completely dried to the crispy stage, like cereal flakes. This usually takes from four days to two weeks, depending on the moisture in the petals and in the air.

If you are in a hurry, spread the petals on a cookie sheet and place them in a warm oven (110° F.). Leave the door open to allow moisture to escape. Stir gently or shake the sheet from time to time so petals will dry evenly. Drying usually takes one to two hours. The flowers are now ready to be turned into potpourri according to one of the recipes below, or your own creation.

The petals are mixed with fixatives to absorb the fragrant oils and preserve the fragrance. Common fixatives include orrisroot, benzoin or storax, calamus powder, violet powder, ambergris, and gum storax. A quarter pound of any one of these is enough for a one-quart potpourri.

To make *dry* potpourri mix the petals with the fixative, add whatever spices and other fragrant materials you wish. Mix well and store in a covered container for several weeks until the fragrances blend and mellow. Then place the mixture in several containers with removable lids. If you use clear glass you have the extra pleasure of being able to see the pretty colors of the contents. Or sew the mixture inside little bags or pillows (sachets) to store inside drawers or closets to keep them sweet smelling. If you choose to keep potpourri in open baskets of wicker or silver, wrap it in a piece of nylon net and tie with a tiny ribbon to keep the petals and spices from spilling away.

Moist potpourris are heavier in fragrance and last longer than the dry type. The slightly dried petals are salted down as in making pickles, with non-iodized salt in a crock, mixed with spices, fragrant oils, and a bit of brandy or perfume. They are stirred together daily for about a month until the scents are well blended and mellowed. It is a good idea to keep a weight on top of the petals while they are mellowing to draw out all the oils from them. If any broth forms, mix it in with the petals.

When the blend is mellow, pour into a large container and mix well once again. Place in small porcelain, silver, or opaque glass containers with removable lids which can be opened whenever you wish to fill the room with the aroma of a summer day. At one time "rose jars" were readily available with double lids—a solid outer, removable one and an inner one with holes to let the fragrance escape. Such jars can be found today in some oriental art shops.

Whenever moist potpourri seems dry and is losing its fragrance, pour a small amount of good quality brandy over the top and mix in to reactivate the fragrant oils. Or moisten the mixture with a homemade rose scent which can be made by placing rose petals in a bottle of wine or spirits. Cork the bottle tightly for three months—then open and add to the potpourri. Enjoy your roses once again!

Moist Potpourri

It is said that this old recipe will keep its fragrance for up to 50 years.

---

1 quart partially dried rose petals
2 cups mixed, partially dried, fragrant garden flowers (jasmine, orange blossoms, lavender, violets)
1 cup dried fragrant leaves
¾ cup bay salt (recipe page 88)
¼ cup crushed allspice
¼ cup mashed cloves
¼ cup brown sugar
1 tablespoon crushed orrisroot
2 tablespoons brandy

1. Mix together the bay salt, allspice, cloves and sugar.

2. Blend the flower petals and leaves with orrisroot. Place some of the petal mixture in a large crock and sprinkle with the salt mixture. Continue alternating layers of petals and salt.

3. Add the brandy. Cap tightly.

4. Open every day and stir.

5. After a month, pour into a large bowl and mix thoroughly. Fill small containers.

Bay Salt

3 broken bay leaves
1 cup non-iodized salt

1. Pour salt over the bay leaves and crush with a wooden mallet or spoon, or with mortar and pestle, until leaves are ground into tiny flakes.

Jackson and Perkins Damp Sachet

1 quart partially dried rose petals
Salt (about ¾ cup)
1 ounce orrisroot or violet powder
Selected crushed spices and herbs
Vanilla beans, broken in small pieces
Perfume, cologne, or vinegar

1. After three days of drying, pack rose petals in jars between layers of salt, adding to each layer sprinklings of orrisroot or violet powder, and, if desired, sprinklings of spices, herb seeds (like caraway, cardamom), herb leaves (like thyme, sweet marjoram, sage, mint, rosemary), and vanilla beans, broken.

2. Sprinkle the contents of a full jar with scent, cologne, or vinegar.

Note: Fragrant oils, powders, leaves, or blossoms of many types can be added to make an even better damp sachet potpourri. A more costly but more long-lasting potpourri of the type may be obtained by adding rose, jasmine, bergamot, lavender, or violet oils.

Caution: Again, prevent mold. Use enough salt to preserve.

American Rose Society's Old-Fashioned Rose Jar

Dried rose petals
Ground cloves, mace, and cinnamon
Fragrant oils such as cedar, sandalwood, jasmine, heliotrope, violet, or lavender
Perfume

1. Place a layer of dried petals in a jar with a tight-fitting lid. Sprinkle lightly with ground cloves, mace, and cinnamon.

2. Add another layer of petals and another of spices, alternating until you reach the top.

3. Add five to ten drops of oil or extract. On the top sprinkle a few drops of your favorite perfume.

Note: If your garden boasts a variety of blooming things, the dried blooms or leaves of lavender, rose geranium, lemon verbena, thyme, or heliotrope can be mixed in with the petals. Your rose jar becomes a potpourri—more interesting to look at, and wonderful to smell.

Jackson and Perkins Dry Sachet

1 quart dried rose petals
1 ounce orrisroot
½ teaspoon *each* cinnamon, ground cloves, allspice, mace, sandalwood powder

1. Blend petals with orrisroot.

2. Make a mixture of cinnamon, ground cloves, allspice, mace, and sandalwood powder.

3. Place a layer of petals in a rose jar and sprinkle with some of the mixture. Repeat the process until the jar is full.

4. Close the jar tightly and store it until all the fragrances have mingled.

Caution: Moldy rose petals ruin the brew. In the dry sachet method, make sure all the petals are *totally* dry.

San Francisco Potpourri

4 cups dried rose petals and small buds
1 cup dried rose leaves
1 cup dried rose geranium leaves
1 tablespoon crushed benzoin
2 tablespoons dried citrus peel
1 tablespoon whole cloves, crushed
1 tablespoon whole allspice
1 teaspoon anise seed, crushed
1 tablespoon cardamom seed, crushed
1 whole nutmeg, crushed
2 bay leaves, finely broken
4 cinnamon sticks, broken into 1-inch pieces
Several drops *each* oils of patchouli, jasmine, rose geranium, and tuberose

1. Place rose petals and leaves, along with geranium leaves, in a large container. Sprinkle with benzoin.

2. Add the spices and mix together gently with your hands.

3. Spoon into selected containers and sprinkle oils on top. Close tightly for about six weeks until the mixture is well aged.

Candles

Roses and candles are both romantic. What better combination could you have?

Paraffin wax blocks or pieces of left-over unscented candles
White string
Rose oil
Food coloring or pieces of wax crayons (optional)
Dried rose petals (optional)

1. Melt wax in a double boiler over low heat. Add a few drops of rose oil and finely crushed petals.

2. Cut string to fit length of mold with a few inches extra. Dip in hot wax. Pull out and straighten to form wick. Tie unwaxed end to a pencil.

3. Pour hot wax into mold (see below). Lower wick into center of mold, hold-ing in place with pencil resting across top of mold. One alternative is to pour the candle, and insert the wick later. This can be done by heating an ice pick, and sticking it into the desired spot in the candle. Then simply put the wick into the hole left by the hot pick.

4. Allow to harden. Trim wick. Remove from mold.

Candle molds: Old-fashioned candle molds are available from craft shops. Or use pâté molds, clean milk cartons, any heavy duty food container, clean tin cans, or make a round mold from heavy-duty cardboard cylinders with thick cardboard bottom secured with masking tape to form an airtight mold. For floating candles, use shallow, individual salad molds. When candles are hard, remove cardboard molds by tearing away. Remove candles from metal molds by running a little hot water over the outside until the candle slips out easily.

Rose soaps

Whether you enjoy taking a brisk shower or soaking in a hot tub, these soaps will make the experience a delight; almost like a walk in the summer rose garden.

Soap from leftovers

Scraps of unscented or glycerin soaps, cut into very fine pieces
Hot water (or hot rose water)
Rose oil

1. Pour hot water over soap shavings in a small saucepan. Add a few drops of oil. Place over low flame and stir until soap is dissolved.

2. Pour into molds and let harden.

3. To remove from metal molds, run a little warm water on outside of mold until soap slips out.

Molds: Use individual salad or pâté molds or wash tin cans such as sardine or tuna cans. Try washed cream or milk cartons which can be torn away after the soap hardens. Then slice the soap into 1-inch-thick bars. Allow soaps to sit for a few days before using. This hardens the soap and makes it last longer.

Old-fashioned rose-scented soap

10 pounds lard
Soft water
4 tablespoons sugar
2 tablespoons salt
6 tablespoons powdered borax
½ cup ammonia
Rose oil (optional)
2 cups lye

1. Spread lard about 1-inch thick on a board in outdoor area. Push roses that have never been treated by any

The essence of fresh roses is an important ingredient in these homemade soaps, dusting powders, colognes, cold creams, and cleansers.

method with any type of pesticides (insecticides, fungicides, etc.), deep into the lard. Cover with cheesecloth to protect from dust. Leave for 24 hours, then remove flowers. For stronger fragrance, add new blooms and leave another 24 hours.

2. After removing flowers, put lard in kettle with 2 quarts water. Bring to boil. Cool overnight. Any foreign particles will sink to bottom and can be scraped off the next morning.

3. Mix sugar, salt, powdered borax and ammonia into 1 cup water. Add a few drops of rose oil, if desired.

4. In outdoor area mix 2 quarts cold water with 2 cups lye in a stainless steel or granite ware pan. Closely follow all precautions and directions on lye label for preparation of lye.

5. Add the sugar, borax, and ammonia mixture.

6. Slowly add cool lard to lye mixture, stirring with a wooden spoon until thick and light in color.

7. Pour thickened soap into stainless steel or granite pan or a wooden box lined with a dampened cloth for easy removal.

8. Leave until soap is hard. The longer you let it dry, the longer each bar will last. Remove from mold and cut into desired portions.

9. Wrapping in soft cloth saturated with rose oil will enhance the fragrance during storage.

Rose Beads for a Rosary or Jewelry

Rose beads are almost extinct nowadays. A few convents still make the beads from bridal roses so the bride can keep part of her wedding bouquet. You may find the ancient art enjoyable. And the little beads will retain their fragrance for years.

Traditional rose beads

1 cup salt
1 cup rose petals, firmly packed
½ cup water
Oil paint (optional)

1. Heat salt and petals, mashing together. Stir in water and add paint for desired color, or leave natural for a brown bead.

2. Reheat, very low, over an asbestos pad, stirring constantly until smooth.

3. Roll out to ¼-inch thickness, cut and roll beads in the palm of the hand to desired shape (oval, round, oblong) until smooth.

4. String the beads on florist's wire or waxed string fastened to a needle. Let dry in a dark place, moving beads occasionally to keep them from sticking.

5. When dry, fashion into jewelry as desired. Wrap in a cloth saturated with rose perfume to increase fragrance.

Note: Should you prefer traditional black rosary beads, cook the petals with a rusty nail, or in a black iron pot with a piece of iron in it.

Bottling the essence of roses

The rose is the most widely used flower of perfumers. Heavily fragrant damask roses of the exotic East are the kind used to extract attar of roses, an oil more costly than gold. It takes 10,000 pounds of petals to make one pound of attar of roses. No wonder those fine perfumes cost so much.

Perfumers obtain oils or pomades, as the solids are known, by steeping the rose petals in a mixture of lard and pure suet. The flowers give up their oils, since oil is attracted to oil.

Here's a simplified way of obtaining a little oil from your roses.

Extracting rose oil

Pour a quart of pure olive oil into a large mixing bowl or crock. Add as many fresh petals as the oil will take. Only use petals from plants that have not been treated with pesticides. Let soak for one or two days.

Then strain the oil through cheesecloth, mashing to squeeze all the oils from the wilted petals.

Once again, add as many fresh petals as the oil will take and let it set another day or two. Strain again. Repeat this process with at least 10-12 batches of petals. Then strain the oil a final time and pour into a bottle with a tight cap.

This rose oil can be added to all kinds of colognes, perfumes, cosmetics, potpourris, and other recipes in this section. Or simply wear the oil alone as a fragrance.

If you do not have enough flowers for this long procedure, rose oil is available from health food stores, herbal cosmetic shops, old-fashioned drug stores, or suppiers of raw materials for perfumers in large cities.

Distilling rose nectar

Rose water has many uses. In Turkey it is a major seasoning, replacing catsup, salt, and pepper. In Egypt it's used as a beauty treatment as well as flavoring for candies, desserts, and drinks. In France it is an eyewash. It is the basic for many cosmetics as well as foods. You'll need to have rose water on hand for many of the recipes in this section.

Here are three methods of securing this nectar of the rose. If you can't find enough roses or time, then you can purchase rose water from gourmet shops, especially those that carry Middle Eastern delicacies.

Select the most fragrant roses available. Only use petals from plants that have not been treated with pesticides. Remove petals and wash well. Cut off bitter white tip from each petal if you plan to use rose water for cooking.

Method I — A simple laboratory. We took 20 feet of copper tubing, rolled it around a heavy cardboard tube to create a coil, which we mounted to a simple 2" x 4" stand with copper wire. (You can also purchase glass coils from scientific laboratory supply houses.) Rubber tubing attaches to a large flask and a small beaker. (See the photo.)

To operate, simply half-fill the flask with two quarts water and two quarts rose petals. (If you plan to use the rose water for fragrances, rather than food, then add 1 quart of pure alcohol.)

Heat the petals and water slowly. We used a hot plate, but you can do it on the kitchen stove. Place an asbestos pad under the flask, and keep the fire on a very low simmer.

Steam rises into the rubber tube, passes through the copper coils where it cools, goes into the receiver flask, which is wrapped in a damp towel and rests in a pan of cool water. An electric fan helps speed up the condensation. Here the steam condenses into rose water.

Method II — Stove-top lab: Fill a regular tea kettle half full of water and cover thickly with rose petals. Attach a rubber hose to the spout and place the other end in a glass jar or bottle on the floor. Arrange the hose so that part of it is submerged in a pan of cold water en route to the jar. Simmer the kettle over low heat. This distillation principle is a simpified process of the preceding method.

Method III — Non-distillation: Use this method only for fragrances or cosmetics—not for cooking. Simply bring two quarts of distilled water to a boil. Remove from stove and add 1/8 ounce rose oil, four drops oil of clove, and one pint pure alcohol. Let stand several days before bottling.

Freshly gathered rose petals are simmered over a low flame to release flavor and fragrance into escaping steam. As the steam passes through the copper coils it is cooled and condensed into rose water.

Cosmetics and colognes

Roses have been a major ingredient in cosmetic beauty secrets since antiquity. Their popularity in cosmetology is mainly for the fragrance imparted to the moisturizers, skin fresheners, and cleansers. Psychologically, it feels clean and refreshing to rub your face with rose petals.

All of the ingredients used in the following cosmetics, colognes, and perfumes are obtainable from old-fashioned drug stores, fancy pharmacies, herbal cosmetic shops, or suppliers of raw materials for perfumers. Check your local yellow pages or ask your druggist for nearby sources.

"Alcohol" refers to 90-96 per cent pure rectified alcohol. It costs more than the rubbing kind, but is odorless and colorless, as it must be for cosmetology.

Simple Rose Perfume

2 tablespoons rose oil
1¾ cups alcohol

1. Mix the oil and alcohol and pour into a clean bottle with a tight-fitting cap.

Note: You can create endless fragrances by adding varying amounts of other floral oils to the above.

Rose Cologne

4 tablespoons rose water
¼ teaspoon rose geranium oil
1 tablespoon spirit of patchouli
⅓ cup spirit of jasmine
¼ cup spirit of rose
1½ cups alcohol

1. Combine all ingredients and pour into bottle or atomizer. Allow to set for at least one week before using.

Note: Homemade floral spirits can be made by adding petals to a bottle of wine, brandy, or vodka and storing for at least three months.

Rose Cleansing Milk

3 tablespoons pure soap flakes
3 tablespoons potassium carbonate
1½ cups hot water
2 tablespoons almond oil
8 drops rose oil
¼ cup alcohol
1 cup rose water

1. Dissolve soap flakes and potassium carbonate in water. Add almond oil. Cool.

2. Dissolve rose oil in alcohol. Add to first mixture.

3. Stir in rose water and pour into jars or bottles.

Rose Water and Glycerin

A famous old, reliable twosome for facial cleansing.

1. Mix equal portions of glycerin (available from your pharmacist) with rose water.

2. Heat just to boiling and store in a capped bottle.

Rose Skin Freshener

¼ teaspoon camphor
1 teaspoon borax
1½ teaspoons tincture of benzoin
1 cup distilled water
½ cup rose water

1. Dissolve camphor and borax in benzoin.

2. Add water and rose water. Mix and bottle.

Rose Skin-toning Lotion

½ teaspoon boric acid powder
4 teaspoons alcohol
2 tablespoons witch hazel
½ cup rose water

1. Dissolve boric acid in alcohol.

2. Add witch hazel and rose water. Let set for one week prior to use.

Rose Cold Cream

4 ounces almond oil
1 ounce white wax
4 ounces rose water

1. Pour almond oil in small saucepan and add wax. Melt slowly.

2. Add rose water a little at a time, beating constantly with a fork.

3. When thoroughly mixed pour the cold cream into jars.

Rose Dusting Powder

1 cup unscented talc powder
1 cup cornstarch
½ teaspoon rose oil

1. Combine the talc and cornstarch thoroughly.

2. Stir in the oil. Let dry thoroughly and put in tight-fitting container.

Cooking with rose petals

Most of us have to develop a taste for rose flavor. A little goes a long way, so it's a good idea to start sparingly. But the addition of rose petals or rose water can change a simple dish into an exotic taste treat.

USE ONLY BLOSSOMS FROM PLANTS THAT HAVE NOT BEEN TREATED WITH PESTICIDES.

Tips for using rose petals in recipes:

1. Select fragrant roses, preferably old-fashioned ones, because there is a relationship between fragrance and flavor.

2. Gently pull petals apart and cut the bitter white tips from the base of each petal.

3. Wash all petals before using.

4. To dry petals for later use, spread on a tray in a warm, arid place until brittle. Stir daily to prevent midew. You can buy dried petals in organic food shops.

5. Ready-made rose water and rose syrup are availabe from some natural food shops, gourmet, or international specialty stores.

Suggestions for using rose water:

✓In ice creams, ices, sherbets.

✓In puddings—bread, custard, rice, or vanilla.

✓In cookies, cakes, candies, frostings.

✓As poaching liquid for fish.

✓As basting liquid for roast fowl and lamb.

✓In eggnogs, sodas, punches, cocktails.

✓In fruit compotes and salads.

Rose Brandy Syrup

1 cup fresh rose petals, tightly packed
1 cup sugar
4 cloves
1 cup water
½ cup brandy

1. Put all ingredients except brandy in a saucepan, bring to a boil; simmer covered for 45 minutes.

2. Allow to cool.

3. Add brandy and strain into bottle or jar.

4. Store in refrigerator until ready to use.

Makes 1 pint.

Rose Butter

Rose petals
Sweet butter, softened

1. Place a layer of butter in the bottom of a crock or jar.

2. Cover with a layer of petals. Continue to alternate layers of butter and petals.

3. Seal tightly and store in cool place or refrigerator for several days.

Blend together just before using. Use on muffins, biscuits, or sandwiches.

Rose Ice Cubes

For festive party punches.

2 dozen miniature roses
Distilled or cooled boiled water

1. Place roses in ice cube trays, one flower per cube.

2. Half fill with water. Freeze.

3. When frozen, fill to top with water and re-freeze. This keeps the roses encased in ice instead of floating to the top.

Rose Bowl

A colonial American recipe.

1 cup Rose Brandy Syrup (page 91)
1 quart club soda, chilled
1 bottle crackling rosé or grignolino
**   rosé wine, chilled**
Rose ice cubes (recipe above)

1. Fill a glass bowl with frozen rose ice cubes.

2. Pour rose syrup, club soda, and wine over the ice cubes. Stir gently.

3. Ladle into individual punch cups.

Note: To make individual servings, fill wine goblet with ice cubes, add tablespoon or more rose brandy syrup. Fill with equal parts soda and wine.

Fruit Punch

2 cups sugar
1 cup rose water
1 cup strong tea
1 cup freshly squeezed lemon juice
1½ cups freshly squeezed orange juice
1 large can pineapple juice
10 ounces frozen strawberries
3 quarts water
1 quart ginger ale

1. Boil sugar and rose water to make a syrup (10 minutes).

2. Add tea and fruit juices. Chill.

3. Add thawed berries and their juice, water, and ginger ale.

4. Pour over rose ice cubes (recipe above).

Serves 30.

Rose Petal Tea

1 to 1½ teaspoons dried rose petals
**   or buds to *each* cup boiling water**

1. Rinse teapot with boiling water to heat.

2. Place rose petals in dry teapot.

3. Add boiling water. Let steep for at least 3 minutes.

4. Strain and serve hot or iced with cream, honey, sugar, or lemon as desired.

Rose Vinegar

1 cup fresh rose petals
1 quart distilled white vinegar

1. Place the petals in the bottom of a quart jar and add the vinegar. Let the jar stand in the sun for two weeks.

2. Strain through a paper filter, rebottle, and seal.

Makes 1 quart.

Note: Vary by using in combination with rosemary, pinks, or lavender.

English Rose Wafers

1 cup granulated sugar
1 cup butter
1 teaspoon nutmeg
Pinch of salt
2 eggs, well beaten
2 tablespoons rose water
2 tablespoons sherry
2 cups sifted flour
1 tablespoon caraway seed (optional)

1. Cream sugar and butter until fluffy. Add nutmeg and salt.

2. Mix eggs, rose water, and sherry. Add to butter mixture.

3. Add flour and mix well. Blend in caraway seed. Refrigerate until well chilled.

4. Work with small batches of the dough at a time. Roll very thin on a floured board. Cut as desired with cookie cutters.

5. Bake at 300° F. until golden brown, about 10-12 minutes.

Makes 6 to 7 dozen.

Note: They keep well for several months when stored in a cookie tin.

Rose Cake

Make as cupcakes or three-layer cake.

1¾ cups cake flour
1 cup sugar
½ cup soft butter
2 eggs
½ cup milk
½ teaspoon salt
1¾ teaspoons double-acting
**   baking powder**
1 teaspoon rose water
¼ teaspoon grated lemon rind
⅛ teaspoon nutmeg or mace
Rose Petal Jam

1. Sift flour and resift with sugar.

2. Add remaining ingredients and beat for 2 or 3 minutes.

3. Bake in greased pans in 350° F. oven for about 25 minutes.

4. When cakes have been in oven about 15 minutes, pull rack out and drop a little jam on top of each cupcake or spread on layer. Return to oven until done.

Frost with Rose Frosting if desired.

Rose Frosting

3 ounces cream cheese
2½ cups sifted confectioners' sugar
1 tablespoon milk
1 teaspoon rose water
Almond or pistachio nuts, finely chopped

1. Cream the cheese with milk, add the sugar gradually, blending well.

2. Add rose water.

3. Spread on cake and sprinkle with nuts.

Rose Petal Jam

1 pound fresh rose petals
2 pounds sugar
Water
1 pound sugar
Juice of 1 lemon

1. Pack petals tightly in a large jar or crock with alternating layers of sugar.

2. Pour enough hot water into jar to cover the petals. Cover with damp cloth for three days.

3. Then prepare a syrup, using enough water to dissolve one pound of sugar before it boils.

4. Cook to soft ball stage.

5. Cook this syrup with the petals and their juices.

6. Let simmer until the mixture is about the consistency of honey. Remove from the stove. Stir in lemon juice.

7. Pour into sterilized jars and seal.

Makes 3-4 pints.

Crystallized Rose Petals

Washed and dried rose petals
Egg white
Granulated sugar

1. Beat egg white to foam and brush it on both sides of petals with a small pastry brush or fingers. Both sides must be moist, but with no excess egg white remaining.

2. Shake granulated sugar on both sides and place carefully on a tray.

3. Dry in refrigerator or a cool room for several days.

Use petals to garnish cakes or eat them as candy.

When you sit down to a tea with everything made from roses, you're suddenly transplanted into an English garden. The three large platters in the foreground feature rose petal sandwiches, English rose wafers, and rosy cupcakes. Toasted muffins are ready to spread with rose butter, rose petal jelly, or rose hip jam. After sipping rose petal or rose hip tea, top off the afternoon with delicate, crystallized rose petals.

Compare the prickly red hips of the English sweetbrier rose (above) with the smooth, bright orange fruit of the hybrid tea (right).

The fruit of the rose

Apples and peaches are members of the rose family, so it should not be surprising that the rose bears fruit, too. The fruit of the rose is the colorful hips. These nutritious little fruits have been used throughout history in medicinal concoctions and remedies.

During World War II, when England was without citrus fruits it was discovered that wild rose hips contained about 24-36 times more vitamin C than equal portions of orange juice and 60 times more of the vitamin than lemons.

Hips are also a rich source of vitamins A, B, E, K, and P, as well as salt, phosphorus, calcium, and iron. Probably no other food produced in the garden even approaches rose hips for concentrated food value.

Hips are produced after the petals fall. In order to have a crop of hips, leave the last blooms of the season on the bush. *Rosa rugosa*, and other shrub species produce the most nutritious hips.

Rose Hip Tea

1 to 1½ teaspoons dried rose hips and seeds to *each* cup boiling water

Prepare like ordinary tea. See Rose Petal Tea, page 92.

Tips for using rose hips in recipes:
1. Use home-grown hips that have not been treated with pesticides, or gather wild hips you know have not been sprayed.

2. Remove blossom ends, stems, and leaves after gathering hips. Wash carefully to remove any insect damage. Chill and store in airtight containers to prevent loss of vitamin C. Use quickly as hips spoil rapidly.

3. To remove seeds from hips, cut the fruit in half and take out seeds, or make a hole in the top and insert a sharp knife to remove seeds.

4. Since the seeds are very rich in vitamin E, it is a good idea to grind them and boil in a little bit of water. Strain through a cloth and add in place of part of the liquid called for in recipes.

5. Vitamin C is easily destroyed by contact with copper or aluminum, so use only stainless steel knives, wooden spoons, and earthenware or china bowls when preparing rose hips. Cook in glass, stainless steel, or enamel saucepans. Always cook quickly and covered, stirring as little as possible.

6. Before drying rose hips, wash and clean them first. Remove seed or leave in. If the weather is warm and dry, spread out on a screen rack until hips are leathery with no moisture left. If climate is cool or humid, dry the hips in a dehydrator or by the sulphur method. (See ORTHO's *12 Months Harvest* book for details of drying methods.) Dried hips can be purchased in organic food stores.

Rose Hip Jam

2 cups rose hips, cleaned
2 cups water
Sugar

1. Cook hips in water until tender, mashing fruit while cooking.

2. Push pulp through a fine sieve.

3. Add 1 cup sugar to each cup pulp.

4. Cook until pulp thickens to jam consistency.

5. Pour into sterilized jars and seal.

Honey of Roses

½ pound rose hips
2 cups water
2 pounds strained honey

1. Mash hips with wooden mallet or spoon.

2. Boil 15 minutes in water.

3. Add honey and boil down to thick syrup.

4. Pour into scalded jars and seal.

Makes about 1 quart.

Fresh rose hips are gathered when they reach brilliant color. They may be turned into delicious syrups or jams, or dried for later use.

Slice the hip open to reveal seeds, which can be removed and discarded, or boiled and strained to secure their vitamin E.

Rose Hip Syrup I

Add a tablespoon of this highly concentrated vitamin source to breakfast juice each day or use in gelatin salads, sauces, or desserts.

Dried rose hips
Water
Sugar

1. Place hips in just enough water to cover. Soak overnight.

2. To each cup of hips and water add ¼ cup sugar. Cook slowly until tender (about 30 minutes).

3. Strain into jars or bottles. Refrigerate until used.

Rose Hip Syrup II

Fresh rose hips
Water
Lemon juice or vinegar

1. Chill freshly picked hips, cut off blossom ends, stems, and leaves. Wash.

2. To each cup of rose hips add 1½ cups boiling water. Cover and simmer 15 minutes.

3. Mash with potato masher or fork and let stand for 24 hours.

4. Strain and bring to a boil. Add 2 tablespoons lemon juice or vinegar to each pint of syrup. Pour into jars and seal.

Rose Hip Jelly

1 quart dried apples
Water
1 quart rose hips
2 cups sugar to each pint of juice

1. Soak apples overnight in enough water to cover.

2. Next day wash rose hips, then cut off calyx.

3. Place hips and apples in a pan with just enough water to cover. Cook until tender.

4. Drain through a jelly bag.

5. Add sugar and boil about 20 minutes, or until mixture jells into a thick mass when dropped from the tip of a spoon into a glass of cold water.

6. Pour into sterilized jars. Seal with wax.

Swedish Rose Hip Soup

1½ quarts water
3 cups fresh rose hips (2 cups dried)
1½ tablespoons potato flour
½ cup sugar
Slivered almonds
Whipping cream

1. Bring water to vigorous boil. Add cleaned rose hips. Cover and cook until tender, stirring occasionally.

2. Strain through fine sieve. Measure 1½ quarts, adding water if necessary, and put in saucepan.

3. Dissolve flour in a little of the liquid and pour into saucepan, adding sugar. Bring to boil, stirring constantly.

4. Pour into tureen or bowls. Add slivered almonds.

5. Serve cold topped with whipped cream.

Rose Hip Wine

2 quarts rose hips
2 gallons water
6 to 8 pounds sugar
½ ounce yeast (2 cakes)
½ cup warm water

1. Dissolve sugar in water and bring to boil. Pour over hips in large crock.

2. When cool, crush hips with wooden spoon or mallet very thoroughly.

3. Dissolve yeast in warm water. Pour over hips and sugar. Cover.

4. Let stand in warm place (65 to 70 degrees F.) to ferment, checking it every few days.

5. When all bubbling stops, fermentation is complete. Strain and let wine stand for at least two weeks.

6. Siphon off the clear part. Bottle and cork.

Note: The longer this wine is allowed to mature, the better. It should be stored for at least one year.